ARTHUR HUGH CLOUGH: A DESCRIPTIVE CATALOGUE

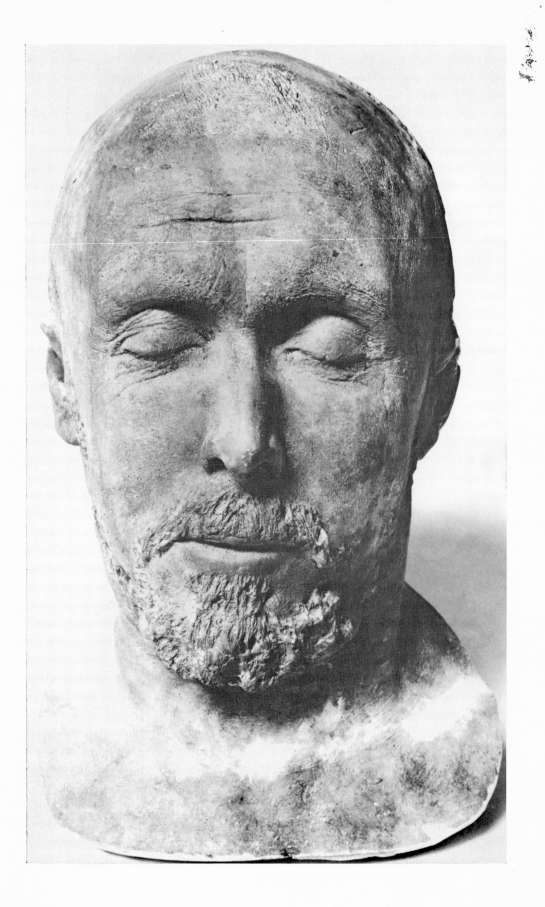

Arthur Hugh Clough: A Descriptive Catalogue

Poetry, Prose, Biography and Criticism

by RICHARD M. GOLLIN,

WALTER E. HOUGHTON,

and MICHAEL TIMKO

The New York Public Library

Astor, Lenox and Tilden Foundations

Library of Congress Catalog Card Number: 67–25798

Copyright © 1966, 1967 The New York Public Library

Reprinted, with additions and revisions,
from the *Bulletin of The New York Public Library*
July 1960, November 1966, January – March 1967
Printed at The New York Public Library
form p745 [xii-28-67 750]

Frontispiece: CLOUGH'S DEATH MASK

Courtesy of Balliol College and the Ashmolean

"I had a cast taken of the head — not very good, but I get fonder of it every day. The features came out so very beautifully after death, though the width of the bone sunk."

— Mrs Clough to C. E. Norton, *C* II 610

Contents

Preface

DURING THE PAST thirty years Clough has begun to emerge from the shadow of a long disparagement. Arnold's condescension gradually became Swinburne's and Strachey's ridicule, and by the 1920s his reputation had reached its lowest point. Yet, though the old attitude persists, he is now finally being recognized as a fine poet, essentially a "modern" poet. This new appreciation is evident not only in articles and reviews, but in six new books: Lady Chorley's *Arthur Hugh Clough: The Uncommitted Mind* (1962); Walter Houghton's *The Poetry of Clough: An Essay in Revaluation* (1963); Paul Veyriras's *Arthur Hugh Clough, 1819–1861* (1964); Michael Timko's *Innocent Victorian* (1966); Wendell V. Harris's *Arthur Hugh Clough* (forthcoming); and Richard Gollin's *Clough's Formative Years* (also forthcoming). By contrast, in the hundred years since Clough died in 1861, he had been the subject of only three major studies. In part this revival has been signaled and made possible by the Clarendon Press edition of his *Poems*, edited by Messrs Lowry, Norrington, and Mulhauser (1951), and by the Clarendon Press selected *Correspondence*, edited by Professor Mulhauser (1957); by making his work available, they have allowed Clough to make his own impact. The scholar, teacher, or reader now needs only two other works: the extensive collection of Clough's prose contained in *Selected Prose Works of Arthur Hugh Clough* (1964), edited by Professor Trawick, and the present Catalogue as supplement to these.

The Catalogue is divided into three parts, devoted respectively to Clough's Poetry, to his Prose, and to Biography and Criticism. Since each has its own introduction, we need only note here that many poems not contained in the definitive edition of 1951 are partly or entirely printed in Part I; that Part II contains a long list of Prose items many of them still in manuscript; and that Part III goes beyond books and articles about Clough to include many references to him from contemporary letters and diaries. Moreover, in all three parts most of the items are described, and in many cases significant quotations from unpublished as well as published material are provided. Such a bibliography will guide and stimulate the future study of a distinguished Victorian.

Though Part I was mainly prepared by Mr Gollin, Part II by Mr Houghton, and Part III by Mr Timko, we have all contributed to each other's work.

Titles of poems or of articles by Clough are given in the list without quotation marks or italics, but such titles are italicized when cited in our introductions or annotations. First lines used as titles, however, are everywhere given within double quotation marks. In some of the listings of tables of contents, single quotation marks designate poem titles which consist of quotations and are set off by quotation marks in the list being transcribed. For example, 'O thou of little faith' ("It may be true") represents a quoted title followed by the poem's first line.

*   *   *

Note: We wish to express our gratitude to Miss Katherine Duff, Clough's grandniece, Professor Mulhauser, and the Bodleian Library for permission to quote from the manuscripts of Clough now in the Bodleian Library; to the librarian of Balliol College, and to Harvard University and the late William A. Jackson, librarian of the Houghton Library, for similar permission to quote from the Clough collections in their archives; and to Professor Mulhauser for making available to us microfilms of Clough's letters and manuscripts in his possession. We must also gratefully acknowledge indebtedness to other institutions and individuals who have variously aided our researches with grants of time, money, knowledge, patience, and willingness to serve: among others to Dr D. M. Barrett, Miss Eva Faye Benton, Mr Kenneth Freyer, Mr Frank Rodgers, and other librarians at Balliol, Bodley, the British Museum, the Library of Congress, the New York Public Library, Pomona, Queens College, the University of Rochester, Rugby, Vassar College, Wellesley College, and Yale University; to M. Paul Veyriras; to Mrs John Conley, Mr Joseph Frank, Professor Wendell V. Harris, Mrs Mary Lefkowitz, Miss Rosalee Szabo, and Miss Barbara Tabak; and to Mrs Richard Gollin, Mrs Walter E. Houghton, Sr, and Mrs Michael Timko; and more recently to Miss Evelyn Barish, Mr Robindra Biswas, Professors Stanley Kahrl and Buckner Trawick, Deans Sidney Axelrad, David H. Krinsley, and Miss Mina S. Rees of the City University of New York, and Dean Lawrence Kuhl of the University of Rochester.

Abbreviations

AHC   Arthur Hugh Clough

Bodleian MSS   Clough Manuscripts in the Bodleian Library at Oxford

C   *The Correspondence of Arthur Hugh Clough*, ed F. L. Mulhauser (2 vols, Oxford 1957)
> There is a useful "Catalogue of all known letters" in II 522–649.

Doct Diss   Doctoral Dissertation

Harvard MSS   Clough Manuscripts in the Houghton Library at Harvard

Letters to Clough   *The Letters of Matthew Arnold to Arthur Hugh Clough*, ed H. F. Lowry (London 1932)

MP   *Modern Philology*

N&Q   *Notes & Queries*

PMLA   *Publications of the Modern Language Association*

Poems   *The Poems of Arthur Hugh Clough*, ed H. F. Lowry, A. L. P. Norrington, and F. L. Mulhauser (Oxford 1951)

PPR   *The Poems and Prose Remains of Arthur Hugh Clough*, ed by his wife (2 vols, London 1869)

PR   *Prose Remains of Arthur Hugh Clough*, ed by his wife (London and N. Y. 1888)

Abbreviations, continued

RES   *Review of English Studies*

RM   *The Rugby Magazine*, which ran from July 1835 to
                    November 1837, in two volumes and eight issues

SPW   *Selected Prose Works of Arthur Hugh Clough*, ed by
                    Buckner B. Trawick (University, Alabama 1964)

TLS   *Times Literary Supplement*

Part I: Poetry

WHAT FOLLOWS is a list, with suitable commentary, of all of Clough's unpublished poems, all of his separately published poems, and all of the editions of his poems — all, that is, that are known to us. It does not include his translations, which remain for the most part in "five half-filled note-books and a bewildering quantity of loose MS. sheets."[1] Nor does it include poems Clough wrote, or may have written, but which do not seem to have survived — e.g. sonnets (other than those in the *Rugby Magazine*) mentioned in his Rugby-Oxford Journals.[2] It has not been possible for us to examine all of the manuscript correspondence for verses his editors may have missed, nor have we had access to the Journals now at Pomona College. But we have listed many items heretofore unnoticed, drawn from collections at the Bodleian and Balliol Libraries, the British Museum, and elsewhere, and present here the most complete descriptive catalogue presently attainable.

A   *Unpublished Poetry*

The following items, numbered 1–37, are a descriptive list of unpublished poems, fragments, or poetical epigrams, and of unpublished stanzas or lines for seven published poems not printed in the notes to *Poems*. The latter are included here because they are of particular interest, because they virtually constitute new poems in themselves, or because they indicate what remains unprinted in the MSS now held in the Bodleian and Balliol Libraries. Where we have made quotations, we have attempted to preserve Clough's spelling and punctuation, but we have sometimes been forced to choose between variant words and lines.

1830 before July 12   "O Muse of Britain teach me now to sing"   *1*

    Eleven heroic couplets lamenting the death of George IV. The poem begins:

> O Muse of Britain teach me now to sing
> In verses sad of our late noble king.
> Teach me in notes of sorrow to proclaim
> To all the world our noble Prince's fame.

---

[1] Quoted from *Poems*, p 582.

[2] In an excerpt quoted by H. F. Lowry, introduction to *Letters to Clough*, p 8. Professor Mulhauser informs us that Journals in his care contain "nine poems or fragments of varying quality" which may not have been published in *Poems* or in *RM*, and may not be among those listed here.

In a letter to his mother, July 12 1830, Bodleian MS Eng Lett c 189, listed as No 7 in *C* II 622. These "verses sad" are apparently Clough's earliest surviving poem. They are preceded in the letter by the statement, "Aunt Harriet requests I will copy the following lines on the late King's death which I made at Rugby."

1837 *July 10*   Snowdon ("Seat of the muse, unrivalled thro the earth")   2

An apostrophe to the "Parnassus of the north" in thirty-seven pentameter couplets, the speaker celebrating its legendary history and identifying himself with its bards. It ends with the chastening reflection that God the maker of Snowdon is the greater majesty. The seventeenth and eighteenth couplets read:

> Ignorance has fled — the harper's wizard hand
> Regains its influence o'er this native land.
> Again to Mona's shores o'er ocean deep
> Sounds of poetic fervour proudly sweep.

MS d 129 fol 79 signed "A. H. Clough, Jesus College, July 10." Fols 75–78 contain two letters to Mrs Clough from Edmund S. Ffoulkes, a nephew by marriage to Clough's "Uncle Alfred," the Fellow and Tutor of Jesus College. The first letter, dated April 4 1862, states that Clough wrote the poem when aged twelve, while vacationing from Rugby at Chester. The second letter, dated four days later, corrects this statement but adds that Clough at that time wrote another poem, now lost, on the Vale of Clwyd. Neither letter is listed in *C*. Clough apparently wrote this poem while staying with his Uncle Alfred at Jesus during the summer just before going up to Oxford.

1839 *May*   "Thou biddst me mark how swells with rage"   3

A six-stanza poem in tetrameters, praising childhood's innocence and joy despite its evidences of supposedly uncontrollable orginal sin. The poem is thus evidence of an early break with one of Dr Arnold's central assumptions, in favor of ("perchance") Wordsworth's in the Immortality Ode. The fifth stanza reads:

> We go our worldly ways, & there
>   Our Eden thoughts we lose them quite,
> Only the quiet Evening air,
>   Or dewy Morn or starry night
> Remind us of the Vision fair,
>   Or bring it back in living might,
> And offer to our tearful gaze
>   The Paradise of childish days

MS d 126 (1839–42 Notebook) fols 9v–10v. A fair copy, dated in the MS.

1839 *before May*   Salsette and Elephanta   3a

The first of Clough's two extant attempts at Oxford's Newdigate Prize (cf *C* I 89–90). This and the item following are poems in heroic couplets, between 250 and 300 lines long, in verse paragraphs of six lines or more. The titles and by tradition the verse forms of Newdigate poems were set by the competition itself. This competition was won by the poem of the same title written by John Ruskin, then at Christ Church.

1840 *before May*   The Judgement of Brutus   3b

For comment see the preceding item. Miss Evelyn Barish, who located these mss, plans to describe them in a forthcoming article.

1839–42 "Irritability unnatural"   4

A brief epigram, probably a metrical experiment, catching a typically Cloughian paradox. Its complete text reads:

> Irritability unnatural
> by slow sure poisons wrought God
>   deaths work, God's doom

MS d 126 (1839–42 Notebook) inside front cover, reversed.

1841 July 28 "About what sort of thing"   **5**

Thirty-six doggerel couplets, apparently written ad hoc, explaining cheerfully to Burbidge that while conducting a Lake District reading party he can find little time to compose poems. He might, for example, write of "Lakes, mountains in plenty,"

> But for them I must trouble you
> To refer to W. W.

In a letter to T. Burbidge, July 28 1841, Bodleian MS Eng Lett d 175 fol 23 and 23v, listed as No 120 in *C* II 625.

1843 after July 1 and possibly before October 14 "And yet, methinks"   **6**

Twenty-six lines of blank verse monologue occupying four pages and following seven which have been torn from the MS. The speaker continues an argument with one "in whom/ The blazing sun hath well nigh drunken up/ All heavenly sap," and who therefore props "the drooping plant/ With the dry sticks & strings of dogmatism." The poem contrasts the life of such a person with one of contemplative, natural growth toward wisdom. The speaker seems to be an early anticipation of Claude, in *Amours de Voyage*. The first lines read:

> And yet, methinks,
> A life, like this, of harmless observation
> Is not without much good — tis this builds up
> I grant you not the hero, yet the sage
> The wise though not the great man; . . . .

MS d 117 (1843 Travel Notebook) fol 29v reversed. Clough began this notebook as a travel diary of a trip to Italy with his close friend Walrond; they met Burbidge in Leghorn and Clough separated from them after a brief illness in Florence, returning to England toward the end of August for six weeks of tutoring in the Lake District (*C* I 125). He began the diary on July 1; the last financial entry is dated October 14, approximately a week after his return to Liverpool.

1844 before November 18 "The Realms of Pure Truth"   **7**

A four-line stanza, written as a metrical experiment, reading as follows:

> The Realms of Pure Truth, Truth irrevealable.
> The Realms of Pure Love, Love beatifical,
> Where thousand thousand Angel Saints praise
> Him that is Truth & is Love, the Most High.

In a letter to T. Burbidge, Nov 18 1844, Bodleian MS Eng Lett d 175 fol 124, listed as No 171 in *C* II 626: The stanza is preceded by the question to Burbidge, "Cans't thou grasp the metrical signification of this —," and is followed by the statement, "I guess you will deny the existence of any metre whatever therein." This letter also contains a translation from Horace.

1844? "Of all thy kindred, at thy dying day"   **8**

An occasional poem in six heroic couplets on the death of a foreigner away from his family, written perhaps for recitation over the foreigner's grave. It concludes by referring to the dead person's family:

> Their hearts so oft have come & sought & seen,
> The Ocean space hath shrunk to nought between
> And now their own seems more the stranger's shore
> Than when with thee they dwelt on it before.

Bodleian MS Eng Lett d 175, fol 71v, listed as No 177 in *C* II 626, where the date is doubtfully attributed. On fol 71 appears the statement, "I do not know whether what I have written on the other side will seem to you to be suited to their purpose, but I wrote them because you said something about it in the Vacation. I think myself Charles' would do as well: & very likely the stone is already put up." Clough's brother Charles apparently also wrote something suited to the occasion.

1845 after August 25 and before November 2   "The Stars that in the East were dim"   **9**

A long meditative ballad about a cottage girl named Janet who returns often to "Ladies well" (a place pleasant in summer and "grave and solemn" in autumn), to sleep and daydream in a wise passiveness. Her "life is emblemed in the stream/ And spring of Ladies well"; it too seems placid, yet is flowing and productive. The poem is Wordsworthian; its use of sun imagery (with "the level ray" coming down "in colours grey" through "the Western Window," and with the quotation which follows) anticipates similar but more significant use of the same image in *Epi-Strauss-ium, Poems*, p 49:

> She slept & dreamt & when she woke
> Thro' Eastern mullions came
> Full sunshine on a face that blushed
> In wonderment and shame.

MS d 119 (1845 Notebook) fols 18–21. Clough began this notebook as a travel diary of a trip through the Lake District and Scotland (see *C* I 149–154 *passim*); its first entry is dated August 25. The poem occurs before a draft of "Oh, ask not what is love, she said," *Poems*, p 11, which Clough copied into a letter of November 2 1845, *Poems* 464–465.

1847   "Fearless over the levels away"   **10**

Nine lines of a poem exhorting himself to "Make for thy self a way," incomplete, ending on variants of a line referring to his "unpolluted" heart: "Though't crack, break it won't."

MS d 120 (1847 Notebook) fols 26–26v, between the first draft of *Epi-Strauss-ium* and the next item.

1847   "The Spirits of the Human Soul that still"   **11**

A rough draft of fourteen whole or variant lines, all cancelled with a single vertical wavy line. It seems to be either a return to the image underlying the 1844 "The human spirits saw I on a day," *Poems*, p 1, or an early anticipation of the 1849 *Bethesda, a Sequel, Poems*, p 53. In this poem the "Spirits" are explicitly aspects of a single soul, and so personify divided attitudes, as in *Dipsychus*. It begins:

> The Spirits of the Human Soul that still
> In individual act & will
> Each with each other fuse & intermingle,
> Chaos, that shifting still conjecture belies
> They several & single
> Took shape before my eyes

MS d 120 (1847 Notebook) fol 27, following *Epi-Strauss-ium* and the preceding item.

1847 September   "Yet wherefore? Were it nothing then, Antaeus-like anew" (additional stanzas for ὁ Θεὸς μετὰ σοῦ)   **12**

A fair copy of forty-two additional lines making up three additional stanzas of ὁ Θεὸς μετὰ σοῦ (*Poems*, p 30); they appear immediately after the additional stanzas given in *Poems*, p 471. The first stanza calls the pious refrain (which is the title and means "God be with you"), a "valediction impotent" since "to bind & not to part/ Fulfills the sole significance of symbols of the heart." The last stanza speaks of an "assurance still mistrusting, which mistrusting still I seek," that he should turn from custom's road back to the lane that leads to the girl's house; this last anticipates Philip Hewson's problem in *The Bothie*. The central stanza is related in many ways to many of Clough's poems. It is quoted here in entirety:

> Thrice blessed, oh, the life wherewith, new blood of strength & health,
> Thy pure & democratic lips endue the child of wealth
> O blessed hundredfold, to hold enfranchised by thy kiss
> The charter, & the freeman's fee of unfactitious bliss:
> Of the lies of breeding, birth, & rank confession made, the grace
> Of absolution plenary to gain in thy embrace;

Thy simple sweet unflattered smile the tincture to remove
All stains upon the tablet where thou writ'st the name of love,
The crucible thy bosom soft wherein the ore misused
May, all its foolish figurings lost, to metal plain be fused —
— Oh benediction insolent! with thee the gift resides
From thee, not me the blessing comes; the life, the force abides,
The justice & the truth with thee; a fact & not a vow
God is, in very sooth, with thee; ὁ Θεὸς μετὰ σοῦ

MS d 129 fols 118v – 121v. For the date see *Poems*, p 470. Similar sentiments in *The Bothie* were declared "indecent and profane, immoral and (!) Communistic," Clough reported to Emerson (*C* I 240).

1847? Homo sum, nihil humani —   13

A ballad in nine stanzas, in the form of statements, questions, and answers, about a man who kissed a girl met on the road "because he knew he could." The first, sixth, and seventh stanzas follow:

She had a coarse and common grace
    As ever beggar showed,
It was a coarse but living face,
    I kissed upon the road.

*   *   *

For royal rich I was of force
    Exuberant of will;
And carnal if she were and coarse,
    She was a woman still.

*   *   *

I kissed, and said, — and piercing-in,
    I looked her through the face, —
I muttered, as I held her chin,
    God give you of his grace!

*   *   *

MS e 88, "Poems by A. H. Clough," being page proofs of the 1849 *Ambarvalia*. This copy contains Clough's corrections of the poems. Before this poem appears the proofreader's sign for "cancel" followed by the words "the whole poem." It appears between ἐπὶ Λάτμῳ and Χρυσέα κλῇς ἐπὶ γλώσσᾳ (the title of which last was added, as the editors of *Poems* note on p 472, on the same MS). "Is it true ye gods, who treat us," in *Poems*, p 43, was apparently then added to fill the space left by this poem's cancellation. It has not since appeared in print. We have not found a MS for this poem; the date is therefore conjectural, based on the poem's similarity to the preceding item. The title is the beginning of Terence's famous line in his *Heauton Timoroumenos*, I, 77: "Homo sum, nihil humani a me alienum puto": "I am a man; I regard nothing that concerns man as foreign to my interests." Here as in *Amours de Voyage*, Canto III, lines 158–159, that which "concerns man" is woman.

1849 ca June 23? Additional verses for "O land of Empire, art and love!"   14

Twelve lines about Rome, originally lines 9–20 of the poem. They do not appear in the later MS followed by the editors of *Poems*:

Was ever seen in tie so close
    With beauty dirt in union?
Did ever glorious things and gross
    Hold such serene communion?
For though for open bridge & street
    I will not feel compunction
Is palace proud a place allowed
    For bestial-filthy function
Must vile expectorations greet
    Angelic limbs with unction,
And marble flags attest the feat
    Of digital emunction

MS d 129 fol 56 and 56v, headed "Now you shall have some sweet pretty verses, in *your* style." A later fair copy, with scatological barbs revised away, is titled "Resignation — to Faustus." Matthew Arnold had earlier asked Clough's opinion of "Resignation. To Fausta." (*Letters to Clough*, p 104). We have given it the date of Clough's only extant letter to Arnold (p 107–109), written when Clough was in Rome; it is in the same mock-irritated mood as the letter, and may have been intended as an inclosure.

1849 *after July 17?*   "O Brien most disconsolate of men"   15

A sonnet addressed to William Smith O'Brien, an Irish insurrectionist who was captured in August 1848 and sentenced to hang, but who was eventually transported and pardoned. The poem refers sympathetically to his "brave delusions" and concludes, "Ireland by thy misjudgement may be taught." Cf Froude's unpublished letter to Clough of August 12 1848, from Ireland (listed as No 305 in *C* II 629), where a sentence reads "It would be a great bit to put Smith O'Brien into an Asylum, and Irish Rebellion is not worth more." Clough nevertheless found his action of moral value, as is seen in the second quatrain:

> Ah be thou well content: no loftier rule
> Stands in the books of Chivalry's high laws
> Than this that bids one for the least good cause
> Risk being thought or even being a fool.

MS "1849 Roma Notebook" (Balliol College Library), cancelled with vertical and diagonal line. This was Clough's travel diary; it shows that he left Rome on July 17, shortly after the French siege was lifted (*C* I 251–273 *passim*). During or shortly after the siege Clough began writing *Amours de Voyage*; the poem on O'Brien appears among some early passages of *Amours*.

1849 *after July 17?*   L[ouis]. XV ("Papers to sign, and documents to read")   16

Fifty-one lines originally preceding the version of *Sa Majesté très Chrétienne* given in *Poems*, p 69–72, and then twenty-one additional lines. In the first of these parts the impotent and weak-willed king tries to assure himself and his children of certain salvation achieved through Roman Catholic rituals; the monologue is addressed to the children. In the second part, addressed to "Monseigneur" of the printed text, the king blames the clergy for his timorous state: they overdeveloped his sense of sin on a single traumatic day, apparently by acquainting him with the facts of sex and the Church's views thereon. The last five lines of this part are spoken by a bystander, suggesting that in this rough first draft Clough was moving from dramatic monologue toward a possible drama. In this MS the psychological bases for the king's theology are much more in evidence than in the printed version. Excerpts from each part follow:

> Come play awhile, & then we'll say our prayers
> E'en as in Church together all
> Say prayers — and then — Which shall it be, you ask
> Ah which.   shall we draw lots? . . . .
>
>   *   *   *
>
> You found me
> A little foolish innocent ignorant Prince
> Awkward & sheepish, bashful & devout
> A silent thinking, somewhat overgrown child
> Who at the coarse-tongued age of [just] 15
> Knew not his sister differed from himself
> Save in her frock & fashion of her hair
> You found me & you told me — Oh kind Saints
> What was it that you told me then . . . !
> But I remember that from that day forth
> The Wicked World was real to me. . . .
>
>   *   *   *
>
>   Tis curious too
> These fits of eloquence that come upon him
> He will go dozing, mumbling [month on month]
> And then at last if something touches him
> Comes out with words like these.

MS "1849 Roma Notebook," after the preceding item, q.v. for the date. This is "MS.1" in *Poems*, p 484.

1849 after July 17? "As one who shoots an arrow overhead"   **17**

A rough draft of seventeen lines, most of them blank verse, on sudden release from strained doubt into total certainty. "Swarth Magellan" finally returns to his point of departure, and that moment, as the last five lines read,

> From far & near
> He drew the scattered ciphers,
> Struck the decisive line, & with one look
> Sum totalled the experience of the World
> In that Augustest Dome. —

MS "1849 Roma Notebook" after the two preceeding items.

1849 after July 17?   Two rejected fragments of *Amours de Voyage*   **18**

Of the many unpublished MS scraps of *Amours*, the following seem of special interest. The first states explicitly one of the lessons Claude fails to learn in time from his experience, and so may guide the many readers who have found the ending inconclusive. (For Claude's somewhat different conclusions see his last letter, *Poems*, p 219–220). The second is from an early draft of the Chaucerian "L'Envoi" to the poem; it contains Clough's accurate prophecy of its reception and evidence that, at least temporarily, he did not find it the poem he had hoped to write:

> It is the virtue of man to know and to love the ideal
> It is the wisdom of man to accept and love the real
>
>   *   *   *
>
> Go, thine epithets earn, morbid, imperfect, obscure
> Go, disappointment that wilt be to friends, disappoint already
> Unto the labouring soul which hath conceived thee and borne.

MS "1849 Roma Notebook," among other passages of *Amours*.

1849–50?   A Highland Love Poem, in Hexameters   **19**

Over 150 hexameter lines of a narrative in which a lowland lad banters with a highland lass who is rowing him across a lake. He takes over the rowing, then delays paying her for the ferry service. It ends with the two sitting together under an umbrella. As the girl's mother appears in the distance the young man finally succeeds in kissing her "over & over." Clough's mastery of dialect rhythms in hexameter can be sampled from the following:

> Answered the lassie to that, Ye're no o' the Highlands yourself, Sir:
> Laddies I'm thinking are idle in Lowland as well as in Highland.
> For in the South, he said, the laddie will row for the lassie
> And in the North, she said, there ha' been laddies to do it.

MS d 124 (Adam and Eve Notebook II) fols 47 reversed — 40v. Unfortunately, of the eight notebook leaves, six have been torn out, leaving only stubs of the lines. The poem appears after a relatively clean copy of part of *Adam and Eve*, which Clough apparently began in 1848 and worked at through 1850 (see *Letters to Clough*, p 86 and *Poems*, p 577). The later date, therefore, is more likely.

1849–50?   In the Sistine Chapel   **20**

A rough draft of nine lines in response to the power of Michelangelo's image of God. Cf Clough's letter of May 24 1849, to Thomas Arnold, Jr (*C* I 256): "I live here studying chiefly Michael Angelo, specially in the Sistine Chapel: I believe the engraving of his Creation of Eve there, more than anything else, led me to Rome. . . . he asserts *totality* — There!" The first eight lines of this unfinished poem are reasonably clear:

> There where He takes His stand
> Upon the ancient half-miraculous clay
> Of the great painter's hand
> What is it He would say?

> The Athlete of the Spirit, the full sum
> Of all perfections to which Earth can come
> There with the thundrous brow & repelling outstretched [hand]
> There as he takes his stand

MS d 129 fol 69. Fol 69v contains random doodlings on the political subjects that pre-occupied Clough during 1849 and 1850.

1849–50? "On which this wild revolving course"   21

A very rough first draft of some twenty-six lines, some cancelled, on the problem of reaching certainty when the cosmos is in continual motion. The central part reads as follows:

> Borne on the mighty cycle year by year
> Of still abandoned still recurrent change
>
> *   *   *
>
> Is there no point where, for one glimpse we see
> Our perfect true condition, own ourselves to be.

MS d 129 fol 36. The date is wholly conjectural, based on the frequency with which Clough returned to this theme during these years; the poem could have been written earlier or later.

1850? "The contradictions of the expanding soul"   22

Forty-five lines of blank verse contrasting the tergiversating and drifting attitude of desiring to "acknowledge brotherhood" and yet fearing "contamination in the jostling street," with the singleminded and high-handed attitude of upperclass scions, who hold themselves frankly superior to their fellow men and so move easily among them. After describing such members of the aristocracy Clough writes:

> The thing that shall replace this is not come
> Earth has not thought it yet: but lying eyes
> Which baffled search the future; on this limb
> This old Historic upgrowth of the Past
> Discern, they seem to think, the woodman's mark
> Who strikes & will not spare. . . .

MS d 129 fols 40, 41 (a clear copy of fols 39 and 39v). A similar idea occurs in a note in the 1850 Venice Notebook, and in drafts of *Amours* and *Dipsychus* written at this time, but the poem's date remains uncertain.

1850 Autumn, or after   "All is not told that might be told"   23

A fifteen line tetrameter poem, rhymed in triplets, on the importance of speaking what "hill & height & wood" fail to speak. Thus it indicates that Clough had moved beyond early Wordsworthian naturalism. It follows immediately after a fine aphorism on arguments from design ("The worst place in the world for finding out what time it is is a Watchmaker's shop"). Some later lines in the poem read:

> And Art outnaturing Nature may
> Articulate the word that hung
> Unsyllabled on Natures tongue
> All is not felt nor said nor sung
> Each has experience of his own
> Which dies if kept to him alone

MS d 133 (1850 Venice Notebook) fol 89v reversed. The poem occurs among drafts of *Dipsychus*, which was "written during or soon after a journey to Venice in the autumn vacation, 1850" (*Poems*, p 528).

1850 Autumn, or after   Three rejected fragments of *Dipsychus*   24

The first of these consists of forty-two lines for Scene xiii in which Dipsychus contemplates roles for himself in the world and satirizes each: student, fop, man of the world, pietist, politician, merchant, lawyer, wit, gentleman, philosopher ("What wilt thou be my soul: —"). The second and third are chiefly given to Mephisto's views on conventional religion ("What if I become your slave, Mephisto, say" and "You'll tell me that my practice goes"). The third shows that Clough was willing to sacrifice wit to decorum when he revised his poems; a revised couplet reads, in *Poems*, p 262:

> I cuff some fellow; mild and meek,
> He should turn round the other cheek.

The MS original read:

> Kick a cad's bottom: mild and meek
> He'll turn we trust the other cheek.

MS d 133 (1850 Venice Notebook) fols 89 reversed — 88 reversed; 28v-28; and 34v-35.

1850–51? "Was it this that I was sent for, do my aspirations mean"   25

A poem in eighteen lines of trochaic octameter couplets expressing impatience with encumbering "petty vulgar doings" such as "Daybooks, ledgers to be posted, hourly pupils taught & crammed." He would rather choose "the instinct . . . of an inward purer mind." The seventh and eighth couplets read:

> O but hunger preaching prudence, O but mouth that must be fed
> And the sick irresolution doubting aye of daily bread
> Is it then so dire to famish, were it worse than once to die
> Or does faith forever cheat us, better voices always lie

MS d 129 fol 64 (a fair copy of the first draft, fol 63-63v). The poem seems to describe his duties and impatience as Principal of University Hall during these years. It might also describe his state at Oriel after 1847, but it contains an image borrowed from Dante's *Divine Comedy,* which he began reading in 1849, too late for an Oriel dating (see *C* I 245).

1850–51? Two doggerel quatrains   26

The first of these looks with wry irony on the positivism of Miss Harriet Martineau, sister of the Unitarian minister whom Clough admired (*C* I 155 and 168), and later translator of Comte (*C II* 469). Clough usually looked upon her with restrained amusement: see, e.g., his comment in 1845; "Miss Martineau is so completely restored by Mesmerism that she is going to write a story for the benefit of the Anti-Corn law league fund" (*C I* 147). The second quatrain looks with equally wry irony on another kind of reformer, the "Chartist tailor"; for Clough's attitude toward this group at this time see Part II, No 33. The two quatrains follow:

> Miss Martineau on evidence
> replaces the abstraction
> With, what in Mesmerism we find
> A sort of spirit action
> The Chartist tailor swears there's come
> One or two revolutions
> At any rate will end all such
> Monarchic Institutions

MS d 138 (*Dipsychus* MS 2 in *Poems* p 529) fol 23 inside back cover. Since this notebook contains very clean revisions of *Dipsychus,* the later date is more likely.

1851 "Within the Frankish ship he came"   27

Thirteen very rough lines, several incomplete, about a stranger in a hostile, bustling city who can nevertheless say "Grace à Dieu" to passers by. It begins:

> Within the Frankish ship he came
> To seek the crowded marts of France
> Of man or thing nor knew the name
> On man or thing nor turned his glance.

MS d 121 (1851 A Notebook) fol 16, following "The grasses green of sweet content," *Poems*, p 392, and preceding the next item.

1851 "Because a lady chose to say"   **28**

Over forty lines (some cancelled) making up three stanzas (the last in very rough form) on the folly of laboring to polish poems only to please "a lady charming fair and young" who had once casually praised them. Friends' compliments are merely formalities, and "It were pollution did we please" the "Vulgar," but this praise has strangely moved him, as the ending of the first stanza declares:

> Is it for this & nothing more
> My brain I ransack o'er and o'er
> And consecrate to make & mend
> Each busy workday's empty end;
> To win some future word's reward
> With labour long & labour hard
> Ah folly folly folly.

MS d 121 (1851 A Notebook) fols 18–19. In the MS this poem precedes "If to write, rewrite, and write again," *Poems*, p 435.

1851 "I said so, but it is not true"   **29**

Thirty-eight lines of tetrameter couplets on the problem of writing exactly "what the soul spoke," the "mere simplicity of what/ We saw," rather than "mechanic substitutes and dead," words that come easily to mind but do not answer the purpose. As the poem says, beginning with the seventh line:

> So perfect, simple & sincere
> So pure & integrally clear
> Behold it into life arise
> And we behold it & it dies
> The vulgar contact of our eyes
> Its volatile pure essence flies
> But in its stead with large supplies
> To shifty understanding brings
> An host of serviceable things

MS d 122 (1851 B Notebook) fols 10v–13.

1851 or early 1852 "Four black steamers plying on the Thames"   **30**

Twelve lines, mostly rhymed, on the repetitive yet busy movement "this side that side up side down side" of four river boats apparently emblematic of human life. Cf his March 8 1851 letter to Shairp, written in a similar mood: "We are still, I believe, travelling about the sun, round and round, and round and round, in the old foolish fashion. . ." (*C* 1 289). The first five lines follow:

> Four black steamers plying on the Thames
> These are their names
> Printed on the paddleboxes any one may know
> Printed up in white
> Morning & evening & Noonday & Night

MS d 129 fol 8, a clean copy of the heavily revised first draft, fol 10. The latter contains a cancelled refrain line, "Paddle paddle paddle paddle paddle." Immediately after this first draft (in a folder entitled "Nursery Rhymes") follows the first draft of "Lips, lips, open," *Poems*, p 106, a part of which Clough sent Miss Smith before early February 1852 (see *Poems*, p 492).

1852–53 or earlier "So still it is, from Reason's throne"   **31**

Ten tetrameter quatrains additional to "What we, when face to face we see," *Poems* p 61, all but the first and last making up together a finished poem of their own of considerable merit. It confronts the central problem of Clough's maturity, how to live in a universe barren of spiritual guidance; it is concerned with mistrust of impulsive feelings, especially in love, and with the hazards of commitment in marriage to a particular person who may not be the divinely intended "elective love"; it reflects worry that we must "see in chance our heavenly choice." The second, fourth, and ninth stanzas follow:

From Reason's pure secluded seat
Sent out into the busy street
To gain experience, we forgo
The faculty by which we know.

*   *   *

We feel; and feelings feelings chase,
Our deepest pains themselves efface.
The lessons that they give to-day
Tomorrow's teaching drives away.

*   *   *

O must we, since, if we would live,
Things must be real and positive,
Take the first plausible pretence
And make it, by our will, be sense?

MS d 129 fol 13 d, a typescript prepared from "MS 3", which is, the MS says, "very rough in places." The notes to "What we, when face to face we see" mention a missing third MS, here found, apparently, too late for inclusion in *Poems*, p 480. The date is approximate, based on dated MSS for "What we, when face to face." That Clough was himself on the verge of marriage at this time need not be significant, since the theme occurs in his poems as early as 1841 (see *Poems*, p 26) and is an especial concern of *Amours de Voyage*, written in 1849.

1852 *between November 15 and November 28* "Lie here my darling; on my breast" 32

Twelve tetrameter quatrains addressed to the spirit of Blanche Smith, later Mrs Clough, imagined present with Clough in America. The first stanza reads:

Lie here my darling; on my breast
I see you so & love you best
Look at me with your glances mild
And play about me as a child

MS d 141 (1852–53 B Notebook) fols 2 and 3. This notebook is titled on its cover "Songs in Absence"; Clough settled into Boston on November 15 and Cambridge on November 24 (*C* II 329, 334). The poem was therefore written, in all probability, between these dates and that of the next item (dated November 28). Clough sent Miss Smith a similar poem ("The mighty ocean rolls and raves," in *Poems*, p 102) in a letter of February 2 1853, saying that he had composed it ten days earlier; see *Poems*, p 491.

1852 *November 28* "Come pleasant thoughts, — sweet thoughts, at will" 33

Another poem for Blanche Smith, in fifteen tetrameter couplets, describing his Sunday blessedness in thoughts of her while "the preacher, much perplext/ Is inking out his weary text." It is addressed to his thoughts, and ends:

I shall be blest, whate'er my lot
So you, — and she, — forsake me not.

MS d 141 (1852–53 B Notebook) fols 4–5. The MS is dated by Clough "Sunday, Nov 28."

1853 *January 25* [28?] "When at the glass you tie your hair" 34

Another poem to Blanche Smith, in eight tetrameter quatrains. This time Clough is with his fiancée in spirit, watching her daily actions, e.g. her sitting down to breakfast or walking in the garden. The first four lines are typical of the whole:

When at the glass you tie your hair
Look out my darling, I am there;
Standing beneath the big oak tree
The moving finger-tips I see.

MS d 141 (1852–53 B Notebook) fols 9, and 9v, dated in the MS. This series to Miss Smith includes as well the poem "Were I with you, or you with me," *Poems*, p 100, and its satirical counterpart, *Poems*, p 401.

1852, after November — or 1853, before July?   The Angel ("Exist — come
    forth —")   **35**

Ten lines, all but the first in blank verse, calling on a Satanic phantom to appear, in God's
name, and perform the divine mission of tempting "this human soul," and thus, by implication,
prove that supernatural powers exist. The last five lines read:

> Go — & as some ill-omened bird of night
> Half-bird, half-beast, with foul & dismal way
> Hover & flit about this human soul
> Flapping thy black temptation in his face.
> While the time, his time & thine — Exist.

MS d 129 fol 59. The date is wholly conjectural, based on the fact that this first draft is
written on the same kind of light blue paper as *O Qui Me* — *Poems*, p 106, which Clough
probably wrote in America (see *Poems*, p 492). But it could date back as far as the drafts of
Dipsychus. Cf the discussion and text given in Katherine Chorley, *Arthur Hugh Clough* (Oxford
1962) 264–266.

1853 ca February 17   Additional stanzas for Last Words. Napoleon and Welling-
    ton   *36*

Two additional stanzas on Napoleon, more bitterly condemnatory than those printed, as
these few lines show:

> Where the fight is — shall we find thee
> Where the corse, thy bird of prey
> Victims still & dupes behind thee —
>   Tête d'Armée

MS d 129 fol 74 and 74v, a party invitation for Thursday, February 17. Clough had
written the main body of the poem by January 4 (see *Poems*, p 488). These stanzas may have
been added when the others were being printed in *Fraser's Magazine* for February of this year
(see below, No 74, and his letter of February 18 in *C* II 381), or they may have been cancelled
from the *Fraser's* version. In the MS, they appear after stanzas three and five of *Poems*, p 93, 94.

1853 before July?   "Nay draw not yet the cork my friend"   37

Twenty-four lines making up four stanzas, in ballad meter, each ending with the refrain
line "Ah no no no not yet." The poem states that "rich exuberance" and "belief", like untasted
wine, should not be expended prematurely. Cf Dipsychus's fear of "adding up too soon," *Poems*,
p 276. The last stanza reads:

> For they shall come that are not now
> We know, tho' do not see
> On them the treasure shall be spent
>   & spent renewed shall be
> On them that are not yet, not yet
> Ah no no no not yet.

MS d 142 (1853 Accounts Notebook) fol 20v reversed, in pencil. Since most of the entries
in this notebook were made in America, perhaps the poem was written there. Clough left America
at the end of June 1853.

B   Poems Published during Clough's Life

Clough's published poems fall into two categories, those published during
his lifetime and those first published posthumously. As the editors of *Poems*
note, both groups contain variant titles and texts, some of them due to
Clough's revision and some to Mrs Clough's. This list gives the titles or the
first lines of the poems — excluding translations — in the order of their

publication or republication, without mentioning variants; these for the most part may be traced by judicious use of the notes in *Poems*. Poems not printed in *Poems* are described briefly; some few poems not positively attributable to Clough are listed with suitable comment.

All but two of Clough's first published poems appeared in the *Rugby Magazine* (1835–1837), signed T.Y.C. or Z, or so attributed in the "Alphabetical Index" to the two volumes compiled apparently by Clough himself (see *C* i 28, 32, and 34; *RM* ii 388; and the comment on Nos 1–13 in Part II). Confirming identification comes from keys to contributors in copies now in the Temple Reading Room at Rugby; these were compiled by H. W. Fox and J. N. Simpkinson, themselves contributors to the magazine. In a copy given to the Yale University Library by an anonymous donor, there appears in faded ink on the last page (*RM* ii 412) a list of the contributors' pseudonymous initials. These are grouped so that T.Y.C., Z, and A.V. (Clough) stand together on the same line, Thomas Burbidge's various initials stand together on another line, and the other initials of other contributors stand separately on lines of their own. The grouping suggests that the compiler of this list had some private knowledge of the contributors. Elsewhere in the two volumes the same hand has written one or another of Burbidge's initials after several otherwise unidentifiable contributions (see, e.g., *RM* ii 387, 398, and 405). On this evidence we have not included these items among those poems that are possibly Clough's.

1835, April 22   The Close of the Eighteenth Century   37A

Twenty Spenserian stanzas describing European history since the Reformation as a "fearful Time" of "Vice and Woe," observing that God's purposes bid Europe to awaken, and ending with a sea image recurring frequently in his later work:

> Lord, we are wandering on an unknown Sea
> Whither we know not; yet we do not fear,
> Though not untroubled doth its face appear,
> And none so far have voyaged there beside,
> So Thou our bark amid its perils steer,
> So Thy invisible pilotage but guide
> The Race of Man through Time — that ocean vast and wide.

A twelve page printed pamphlet (Rugby 1835) in the British Museum, attributed to Clough in ink on the title page, which reads *The Close of the Eighteenth Century, a Prize Poem, Recited in Rugby School, Wednesday, April 22, 1835.* It is also attributed to Clough in the bound volume of prize poems kept at Rugby School; and see Clough's comment on it in *C* i 32. Not printed in the *Rugby Magazine*, nor since.

1835 July   The Poacher of Dead Man's Corner; or, the Legend of Devil's Turning,
   RM i 35–43. Signed T.Y.C.   38

A long folktale in fourteeners, tetrameter couplets, and quatrains, occasionally mocking its own foreboding tone, about a cheerful poacher who suddenly encounters a ghostly, moonlit procession of his family. He returns home and there (while "The embers' flame burnt green and low,/ And scarce its flickering light could show") finds his family dead. He takes to his bed and himself dies.

——— ——— The First of the Dead, *RM* i 62–63. Signed T.Y.C.   **39**

An elegy in fourteeners on the death of a girl, apparently a sister, and the consolation of eternal life (". . . we mourn thee as a flower/ That hath but closed at eventide to wait the morning hour").

——— *October*   Count Egmont, *RM* i 160–162. Signed Z; indexed T.Y.C.   **40**

A ballad in fourteeners in the manner of Macaulay's "Battle of Ivry," on which Clough had just written an article (see Part II, No. 3). Having fought to free his country and now about to be executed, Count Egmont considers calling on a sympathetic crowd to liberate him, realizes that this would only bring his doom upon them, reconciles himself to his death, and dies anticipating heaven.

——— ——— "O Moon, and stars, and sky! at every tide," *RM* i 173–174. Signed T.Y.C.   **41**

A sonnet on the heavens' reflection of divine love and sympathy, where "Our weaker visions by faint glimpses see/ The tie that links those million worlds together."

——— ——— "O Heaven, and thou most loving family," *RM* i 175. Signed T.Y.C.   **42**

A sonnet contrasting the loving sympathy of the stars with the speaker's gnawing sense of guilt. This and the preceding item appear in a group of five sonnets with a prose introduction entitled "The Lunar Microscope," and indexed T.Y.C. The other sonnets were provided by other contributors. Cf Dipsychus' address in *Poems*, p 229.

1836 January   "I watched them from the window, thy children at their play," *RM* i 308–309. Unsigned; indexed T.Y.C.   **43**

Given in *Poems*, p 437f. Its nostalgia is tempered by the editorial comment, probably Clough's, which follows it: " 'Enough, enough,' cried the editor, after a yawn." Mrs Clough provided the title *Thoughts of Home* for *PPR* ii 2.

——— ——— The song of the Hyperborean Maidens, *RM* i 309–310. Unsigned; indexed T.Y.C.   **44**

Six stanzas of anapestic tetrameters, sung by the maidens in "Herodotus, IV, 33" (as a headnote observes) , as they bring gifts to "the Lord of the South" and "the Lady of Night."

——— *April*   To ———, On Going to India, *RM* i 320–322. Signed T.Y.C.   **45**

Eight stanzas taking leave of a departing friend, recalling shared scenes and experiences, and giving assurance that God will continue to watch over both of them: "Yea, sky and stars may change with sea and shore,/ But he abideth forever, ..." Cf *Qua Cursum Ventus* and *Sic Itur*, *Poems*, p 34 and p 7, both written less than ten years later.

——— ——— The Old Man of Athens, *RM* i 399–400. Unsigned; indexed T.Y.C.   **46**

A poem in fourteeners in which an Old Athenian decides it is time for him to die; he has viewed Athens in its greatness, outlived the glories of war and philosophy, and having thought the light of wisdom permanent, has found that it is not.

——— ——— The Exordium of a Very Long Poem, *RM* i 404–405. Unsigned; indexed T.Y.C.   **47**

Printed in *Poems*, p 438. After the last stanza appears the editorial statement, "The rest is happily wanting."

1836 June   The Longest Day   **48**

A poem in five stanzas of ten lines each, first celebrating the light and triumph of the sun at the summer solstice, then asking "Is there no note sobering sadness/ In that thy proud and swelling sound," then fiinding it in the fact "That each day now will be more brief," then concluding:

> . . . summer flowers may cease to blow,
> And summer suns less brightly glow,
> But Goodness never, never fadeth,
> And Love's bright sun no winter shadeth. . . .

A privately printed, five page pamphlet in the British Museum, the title page attributing it to Clough and reading *The Longest Day, A Poem written at Rugby School, Fourth Lesson, Wednesday, June, 1836,*" n. p. This poem was not printed in the *Rugby Magazine*, nor has it been reprinted since.

—— *July*   Lines, *RM* II 74–76. Signed T.Y.C.   **49**

Printed in *Poems*, p 439. Mrs Clough changed the title to *An Evening Walk in Spring* for *PPR* II 5.

—— ——   An Apology, *RM* II 96–98. Unsigned; indexed T.Y.C.   **50**

Ten stanzas pointing out in the refrain line of each that because Spring has charmed him, he "cannot write a single word," the last two whimsically and then piously pointing out the absurdity of a poem written about one's inability to write.

—— *December*   An Answer to Memory, *RM* II 132–135. Signed T.Y.C.   **51**

Five fourteen-line stanzas replying to J. N. Simpkinson's "Memory," a poem in nearly the same stanzaic form which had argued on the preceding pages for past emotion recollected in tranquility. This poem argues on the other hand that present experience precipitated spontaneously into language makes better poems.

—— ——   An Incident, *RM* II 135–136. Signed T.Y.C.   **52**

Printed in *Poems*, p 441.

1837 July   A Peripateticographical Article, *RM* II 223–234. Unsigned; indexed "T.Y.C. &c."   **53**

This article (see Part II, No 10) includes seven poems in appreciation of the Rugby countryside — the Avon, and hedgerows, for example. None is clearly identifiable as Clough's, but two of them bear especially close resemblance to other Clough poems: *To Certain Elm Trees* (like "An Incident," No 52) describes a Wordsworthian spot of time; and "They came in crowds, but I meanwhile" is similar to Clough's later "— Roused by importunate knocks."

—— ——   Epilogue to the Sonnets, *RM* II 284–285. Unsigned; indexed T.Y.C. **54**

Following Clough's article *Sonnets in the Abstract* (See Part II, No 11) and Burbidge's sixteen "Sonnets in the Concrete," this poem in three stanzas comments appreciatively on the latter.

—— ——   April Thoughts (No 2), *RM* II 294. Signed Z; indexed T.Y.C.   **55**

Three stanzas of ottava rima grieving because, having slighted "Beauty, Truth, and Goodness," he is too depressed to respond to the signs of oncoming summer.

—— *November*   Verses from the School-House, *RM* II 346–348. Unsigned; indexed T.Y.C.   **56**

A poem in fourteeners recalling his eight years at Rugby, and especially the death of a school-fellow. Six years afterward the speaker saw the boy's name carved in a desk; the sight brought on a mood of chastened solemnity. So thoughts of the dead boy can lessen future heedless moods.

—— —— Rosabel's Dream, *RM* II 361–374. Unsigned; indexed T.Y.C.   **57**

A long ballad, obviously imitating "Christabel," about a medieval girl who is troubled by evil temptations in her dreams, awakens anguished and penitent, and finally sinks into untroubled sleep hearing a voice assure her of divine aid.

—— —— The Effusions of a School Patriarch, *RM* II 389–390. Unsigned; indexed T.Y.C.   **58**

Given in *Poems*, p 443. The note to this poem (p 581) mistakenly ascribes it to the issue of July 1837. This and the remaining *Rugby Magazine* items appear in the article "Conclusion" (*RM* II 388–405), indexed T.Y.C. and F.D.A. (Burbidge).

—— —— Bores, *RM* II 390–391. Unsigned and not separately indexed.   **?59**

A high-humored recounting of the minor annoyances of Rugby life, like the preceding item both amusing and nostalgic in tone. It may not be Clough's, but is listed here because of prefatory editorial dialogue linking it to the preceding item: "Never was anything so preposterous!" "I beg your pardon — lo! I will mate and match it blissfully!"

—— —— "I love to see the Sun Arise," *RM* II 393. Unsigned and not separately indexed.   **?60**

A poem speaking of "soul-felt happiness" when the sun and — toward the end — stars seem to give evidence of a harmonious "universe of love." It may not be Clough's, but is listed here because the imagery is similar to that of several poems already described, and because it occurs in an editorial soliloquy by Clough.

—— —— "Oh, the sweet botheration of sweet No. 1!," *RM* II 394. Unsigned and not separately indexed.   **61**

Doggerel reminiscences about the first issue of the magazine. It is unsigned, but probably Clough's: it occurs in the same editorial soliloquy mentioned in the previous item, preceded by the statement "Here the delights of No. I . . . seemed to burst upon him, and he [i. e. Clough] enthusiastically broke out into the following exclamatory song. . . ."

—— —— To a Crab Tree, *RM* II 397. Signed Z; indexed Z.   **62**

A poem describing a crab-apple tree which once flowered beautifully but now produces only "sour useless fruit," hoping that the tree does not figure forth his own career.

1838 June   A Stray Valentine, *Youth's Literary Messenger* II (June 1838) 52   **63**

A sonnet on the lovely connotations of various girls' names, ending:

> But one dear name there is, — not all unknown
> To poet's lofty strain, — whose silver tone
> Brings me the image of a fair, bright bride,
> And makes my tingling blood beat fast and high;
> Oh, all the rest may perish, so but I
> In the soft light of Lucy's love abide.

Clough sent this poem and the one following to his sister Anne in a letter dated October 15 1837 (listed as No 60 in *C* II 624). *Youth's Literary Messenger* was a short-lived American periodical; there is a file in the Library of Congress. Both poems were printed anonymously, but both are signed "Oxford, Eng." and "Rugby"; Clough had just settled in at Balliol. Neither has been reprinted.

—— —— Verses, Written in a Diary, *Youth's Literary Messenger* II (June 1838)
65–66   **64**

Fourteen quatrains in ballad meter on the theme that while "Another day has past away/ No better than the last," there is consolation that the sun's "holy light shall stream/ On all thy path behind" when it finally rises, no matter how dark things ahead seem to look. Clough often employed this image, but the ninth and tenth stanzas especially forecast its use in "Say not the struggle":

> At eve upon a western road,
>   Say! hast thou never seen,
> How bright the skies in distance glow'd,
>   How dark the things between,
>
> How black the gate, the field, the hedge,
>   The steeple slim and high?
> The tall trees, on the green slope's edge,
>   Stood out against the sky.

For the attribution see the previous item.

1846 January 30   I Give Thee Joy, *The Balance*, p 36. Signed O.A.M.   **65**

Entitled *In Faith, Nothing Wavering* in the 1850 reissue of *Ambarvalia*, but not since. Printed in *Poems*, p 3. For the attribution to Clough see *C* ɪ 169.

—— *February 13*   Differ to Agree, *The Balance*, p 55. Signed O.A.M.   **66**

See the preceding item. Entitled *Sic Itur* in the 1850 reissue of *Ambarvalia*, and since. Printed in *Poems*, p 7.

1847 "See! the faint green tinge from the western sky. . . ," in "Illustrations of Latin Lyrical Metres," *The Classical Museum* ɪv (1847) 352. Signed A. H. Clough
67

Eight lines of what Clough calls (with the next item) "quasi-nonsense verses [which] do their utmost to preserve in their strongest character Horace's favorite central molossi," evoking the stillness and sad isolation felt in the presence of oncoming evening. Matthew Arnold's "Dover Beach" may be reminiscent of the second stanza:

> Now, in this deep stillness from tower and steeple
> Hark! the long loud knell! to the hills it past, and
> List! the same sad sound from across the wide bay
>   Faintly re-echoed.

This and the next two items appear among translations, chiefly of Horace, illustrating a theory of metrical translation: see Part II, No 19, and *C* ɪ 142, where it appears that the three items were written before December 31 1844; and see Part I, No 7 above.
They have not been reprinted.

—— ——   "— So he/ Journeyed and came to /Horeb. . . ," in "Illustrations of Latin Lyrical Metres," *The Classical Museum* ɪv (1847) 352   **68**

Seven lines on Moses' journey to Horeb, where he encountered wind, tempest, flame, and finally "a still small voice." It has not been reprinted. Cf No 67.

—— ——   "Down to the Derwent hurry the Greta, the Glenderaterra," in "Illustrations of Latin Lyrical Metres," *The Classical Museum* ɪv (1847) 358   **69**

Eight lines describing in carefully articulated rhythms the course of streams in the Lake District from their "thousand rills" to "their ultimate ending" in the ocean. It has not been reprinted. Cf No 67.

1848 November   The Bothie of Toper-na-fuosich, a Long-Vacation Pastoral (Oxford and London 1848)   **70**

This narrative poem "in about 2000 hexameters" (*C* I 224) was written rapidly during the preceding two months (*C* I 240); an American edition followed in 1849. For comment on the texts of subsequent editions, all posthumous, see *Poems* 496–497.

Early in 1849 Clough was amused and embarrassed to discover that the latter part of the title, which he had drawn from a map, was in fact Gaelic for a bawdy Highland toast to womankind (meaning "the bearded well"): see *C* I 244; and *N & Q*, 5th Series, August 4, September 8, November 17, and December 1, 1877, and February 9, and March 9, 1878. When a new American edition was proposed in 1855, he improvised the title the poem has since held, *The Bothie of Tober-na-Vuolich* (*C* II, 505, 514).

1849 The Bothie of Toper-na-Fuosich, a Long-Vacation Pastoral (Cambridge, Mass 1849)   **71**

An exact reprint of the above.

1849 January Ambarvalia (London and Oxford 1849) p 1–64 (no preface or table of contents)   **72**

The following is a list of the poems Clough selected for the only collection published during his lifetime, all of them written during the preceding decade (see *C* I 240) and published together with poems by his friend Thomas Burbidge. The list includes "I give thee joy!" (No 65) and "As, at a railway junction" (No 66), but no other previously published poems, and not the printed but cancelled poem *Homo sum, nihil humani* (No 13).

For the complex history of the texts in this volume, and their dates, see *Poems* p 457. As Charles Eliot Norton wrote in Longfellow's copy (now at Harvard), "Ambarvalia had but small sale, and Clough, separating his poems from those of Burbidge, had copies of them done up by themselves, for gifts to his friends." One such copy (1850), with revisions, is here (as in *Poems*) called *Reissue A*; another (1853) is called *Norton Reissue*. The titles Clough provided some of these poems in *Reissue A* are apparently the last authorized; Mrs Clough's titles in the posthumous editions differ from these unless otherwise noted. In 1858 (*C* II 560–562), Clough sent Norton a list of *Ambarvalia* poems for reprinting in a projected volume of his verse, including revisions and three additional title changes; Mrs Clough retained these titles. *We have placed an asterisk after those items Clough intended for the projected volume, and a double asterisk after those items he added on Norton's recommendation* (*C* II 565).

Here as wherever a table of contents is given in Part I, a poem with a Greek title or with a title that might not identify it in *Poems* is further described in parentheses. Since the poems listed in these tables of contents are all reprinted in *Poems*, we have not thought it necessary to number them separately.

"The human spirits saw I on a day" (titled *Through a Glass Darkly* in *Reissue A*, then in 1858 *The Questioning Spirit*) *

"Ah, what is love, our love, she said" (titled *Flet Noctem* in *Reissue A*)

"I give thee joy! O worthy word!" (titled *In Faith, Nothing Wavering* in *Reissue A*)

"When panting sighs the bosom fill"

"As, at a railway junction, men" (titled *Sic Itur* in *Reissue A*, and thereafter) *

Commemoration Sonnets. Oxford, 1844. (The first two were omitted in *Norton Reissue*)

I   "Amidst the fleeting many unforgot"

II   "Thou whom thy danglers have ere this forgot"

III   "Not in thy robes of royal rich array" (titled *A Royal Visit* in *Reissue A*, and *The King of Saxony's Visit* in *Norton Reissue*)

"Come back again, my olden heart! — " *

"When soft September brings again" *

"Oh, ask not what is love, she said"

"Light words they were, and lightly, falsely said:"

Qui laborat orat

"With graceful seat and skilful hand" (title *Contemplator* Θεατής in *Reissue A*, then alternatively in 1858, *In a Drawing Room*) *

When Israel came out of Egypt (titled in 1858 *The New Sinai*) *

"The Silver Wedding! on some pensive ear"

I   "Why should I say I see the things I see not"
II   "Are there not, then, two musics unto men?"
III   "Yea, and as thought of some beloved friend"
"Sweet streamlet bason! at thy side" (an alternative title in 1858 was *The Clouded Hill*) *
"Away, haunt not thou me" (titled in 1858, together with the next item, *In a Lecture Room*) *
"My wind is turned to bitter north." **
"Look you, my simple friend, 'tis one of those" (titled *The Poet* in Reissue A)
"Thought may well be ever ranging" (titled *Duty-Love* in Reissue A)
"Duty — that's to say complying"
'Blank Misgivings of a Creature moving about in Worlds not realized"
I   "Here am I yet, another twelvemonth spent"
II   "Though to vilest things beneath the moon" *
III   "Well, well, — Heaven bless you all from day to day!"
IV   "Yes, I have lied, and so must walk my way"
V   "How often sit I, poring o'er"
VI   "— Like a child"
VII   "— Roused by importunate knocks" **
VIII   "O kind protecting Darkness! as a child" *
IX   "Once more the wonted road I tread"
X   "I have seen higher holier things than these"
Qua cursum ventus *
Alcaics ("So spake the Voice: and, as with a single life")
Natura naturans *
ὁ Θεὸς μετα σοῦ ("Farewell, my Highland lassie!")
ἐπὶ Λάτμῳ ("On the mountain, in the woodland") *
Χρυσέα κλὴς ἐπὶ γλώσσᾳ ("If, when in cheerless wanderings, dull and cold")
"Is it true, ye gods, who treat us"

1850 Poems by Arthur H. Clough (n. p., n. d.)   **73**

The 1850 reissue of Clough's poems in *Ambarvalia*, described in No 72.

1853 February Last words. Napoleon and Wellington, *Fraser's Magazine* XLVI (February 1853) 155–156   **74**

Printed in *Poems*, p 93. Clough felt that the first part was composed too rapidly (*C* II 381), and added two more stanzas perhaps afterwards (see above, No 36).

—— *May* "As ships, becalmed" (*Qua cursum ventus*) reprinted in the anthology *Thalatta: a Book for the Sea-side*, ed S. Longfellow and T. W. Higginson (Boston 1853) p 205   **75**

The text was taken from *Ambarvalia*. Clough's is the last poem in the collection; for his reaction see *C* II 429.

—— *July* "Upon the water in a boat," *Putnam's Magazine*, II (July 1853) 72 **76**

This and the next three items appeared in Clough's two "Letters of Paripedemus" (see Part II, Nos 56–57), written perhaps at James Russell Lowell's urging (*C* II 378). There they served as poetical extensions of his discussion. Printed in *Poems*, p 108.

—— —— "To spend uncounted years of pain," *Putnam's Magazine* II (July 1853) 73   **77**

Mrs Clough apparently drew this poem's later title, *Perchè pensa? Pensando s'invecchia*, from the discussion immediately preceding this poem's presentation. Printed in *Poems*, p 90.

—— —— "In vain I seem to call, and yet," *Putnam's Magazine* II (July 1853) 74

This is the last stanza of "Come, Poet, come," *Poems* p 108.   **78**

—— *August*   "My dear sir, here is a chapter. . . ." *Putnam's Magazine* II (August
1853) 140   **79**

Printed in *Poems,* p 586.

1854 May   Peschiera, *Putnam's Magazine* III (May 1854) 522   **80**

Printed in Poems, p 72. For Clough's comment see *C* II 478.

1855 August   The Struggle ("Say not the Struggle nought availeth"), *The Crayon*
II (Aug 1 1855) 71   **81**

This first publication in a reputable American art journal was first noted by F. G. Townsend in 1952 (Part III, No 387); he is unable to assert that the title is Clough's.
Printed in *Poems,* p 63. (Also see Part III, Nos 374, 395, 416.)

1858 February through May   Amours de Voyage, *The Atlantic Monthly* I (1858)
as follows: **82**

Canto I, February, 419–426; Canto II, March, 536–543; Canto III, April, 667–673; Cantos
IV and V, May, 784–790.
For the textual history of this "5 act epistolary tragi-comedy or comi-tragedy" in hexameters (*C* II 546) see *Poems* 512–513. Clough began it during the siege of Rome in mid-1849,
and started showing it to his friends in November of that year. Their responses were disappointing: see, e.g. *C* I 275–278, and *Letters to Clough,* p 132. He worked further at it in 1850, then
in 1854 mentioned its existence to Norton (*C* II 482). In 1857 J. R. Lowell accepted it for *The
Atlantic* (*C* II 536–537), where it was published, in *The Atlantic's* manner, without attribution.
As Clough anticipated, friends found the ending disappointing (see Emerson's letter in *C* II 548),
and finally his own confidence in the poem was somewhat shaken (*C* II 543, 546, 547, 551, and
552).

C   Posthumous Publications

Clough died on November 13 1861, before most of his short poems, his
dramatic poems *Dipsychus* and *Adam and Eve* (called, in *Poems, The Mystery of the Fall*), and his long narrative poem *Mari Magno* had been published. He seemed to have accomplished little, as friends observed to his
widow (C II 604–606). But two weeks after his death Mrs Clough wrote
Norton about a British and American edition of his works, and in a month
the project was under way (*C* II 609, 612). The next five items resulted; see
Poems, p 473, for additional bibliographical details.

1862 Poems by Arthur Hugh Clough (Cambridge and London, 1862), with a
memoir by F. T. Palgrave   **83**

On the memoir, see Part III, No 85; see also below, Nos 93 and 94.
This edition follows, for the most part, Clough's instructions to Norton about selections
of poems from *Ambarvalia* (*C* II 561–562, and 565). It leaves out, apparently contrary to Clough's
instructions, the *Commemoration Sonnets,* "With graceful seat and skilful hand," and *Natura
Naturans.* On the other hand, it includes the following poems Clough considered excluding:
"When panting sighs. . . ," "Are there not, then, two musics. . . ," "Yea, and as thought. . . ,"
"Thought may well be ever ranging," "Duty — that's to say complying," 'Blank Misgivings . . .'
III, V, and VI, and "If, when in cheerless wanderings. . . ." The poems of 'Blank Misgivings'
(excluding I and IV) are printed without indication that they were once part of a group. Four
Mari Magno tales are included, without indication that there were others. As the following table

of contents shows, most of the poems were still without titles, and eleven selections from *Dipsychus* were printed under the titles *At Venice* and *Spectator ab extra*, or by themselves untitled:

"Come back again, my olden heart!"
"When soft September brings again"
"Sweet streamlet bason! at thy side"
In a Lecture Room ("Away, haunt thou not me")
"Though to the vilest things beneath the moon"
"Well, well, — Heaven Bless you all from day to day!"
"How often sit I, poring o'er"
" — Like a child"
" — Roused by importunate knocks"
"O kind protecting Darkness! as a child"
"Once more the wonted road I tread"
"My wind is turned to bitter north"
"I have seen higher holier things than these"
"If, when in cheerless wanderings, dull and cold"
"Duty — that's to say complying"
"Are there not, then, two musics unto men" (consisting of two parts as follows)
   I   "Are there not, then, two musics unto men"
   II "Yea, and as thought of some beloved friend"
"Thought may well be ever ranging"
"When panting sighs the bosom fill"
ὁ θεὸς μετὰ σοῦ ("Farewell, my Highland lassie!")
"Light words they were, and lightly, falsely said"
Sic itur
Qua cursum ventus
The new Sinai ("Lo, here is God, and there is God!")
The questioning spirit ("The human spirits saw I on a day")
Bethesda: A Sequel
"Across the sea, along the shore"
The song of Lamech
Jacob
At Venice
   On the Lido ("On her still lake the city sits") [*Dipsychus*, Scene V, 197–200]
   In the Piazza at night
      "Oh beautiful beneath the magic moon" [*Dipsychus*, Scene IX, 12–23]
      "My mind is at rest; my heart at home" [*Dipsychus*, Scene X, 72–84]
      "Come, leave your Gothic worn-out story" [*Dipsychus*, Scene IV, 204–223]
Spectator ab extra [*Dipsychus*, Scene IV, 130–195, in the earlier version printed in *Poems*, p 539–542]
The Latest Decalogue
"'There is no God,' the wicked saith" [*Dipsychus*, Scene V, 154–185]
"Submit, submit!" [*Dipsychus*, Scenes IX, 160–184; X, 164–170; XI, 87–104, 199–213]
"When the enemy is near thee" [*Dipsychus*, Scene XII, 8–31]
"Hope evermore and believe, O man, for e'en as thy thought"
"What we, when face to face we see"
Peschiera
Alteram Partem
"Say not, the struggle nought availeth"
Ite domum saturae, venit Hesperus ("The skies have sunk, and hid the upper snow")
"'Old things need not be therefore true'"
"O Thou whose image in the shrine"
"It fortifies my soul to know"
"Where are the great, whom thou wouldst wish to praise thee" [*Dipsychus*, Scene IV, 122–127]
"Come home, come home, and where is home for me"
"Green fields of England! wheresoe'er"
"Come back, come back, behold with straining mast"
"Some future day when what is now is not"

"Where lies the land to which the ship would go?"
"The mighty ocean rolls and raves"
"That out of sight is out of mind"
"Were you with me, or I with you"
Qui laborat, orat (inserted here in the table of contents, but actually appearing in the
    volume after *Qua cursum ventus*)
"How in Heaven's name did Columbus get over"
To a sleeping child ("Lips, lips, open!")
"O stream descending to the sea"
"Put forth thy leaf, thou lofty plane"
"Trunks the forest yielded, with gums ambrosial oozing"
"Come, Poet, come!"
THE BOTHIE OF TOBER-NA-VUOLICH
AMOURS DE VOYAGE
MARI MAGNO, OR TALES ON BOARD
    Preface
    The Lawyer's Tale (*Edmund and Emma*)
    My Tale
    The Clergyman's Tale (*Edward and Jane*)

1862 The Poems of Arthur Hugh Clough (Boston 1862), with a memoir by Charles
        Eliot Norton   *84*

On the "Memoir" see Part III, No 84.
    This edition is similar to the English. It omits "My mind is at rest; my heart at home"
from *At Venice*; it adds "Blessed are those who have not seen"; and it prints a few poems in
slightly different order (e. g. "Old things need not" precedes rather than follows *Ite Domum*,
and the long poems begin rather than end the volume). Three sonnets are so called in the
table of contents.

1863 Poems by Arthur Hugh Clough, Second Edition (London and Cambridge
        1863), with a memoir by F. T. Palgrave   *85*

The memoir is that of 1862, slightly revised. The order is somewhat rearranged from the
first English edition; "How in Heaven's name did Columbus get over" is omitted; *Edmund
and Emma* (from *Mari Magno*) is attributed to the clergyman rather than the lawyer; *Primitiae* and *Christian* are added to *Mari Magno*, attributed to the lawyer, and *The Mate's Story*
is added as well; and the following new poems appear:

"When the dews are earliest falling"
"O tell me friends, while yet we part"
"Upon the water, in a boat"
"Each for himself is still the rule"
"Whence are ye, vague desires"
"On grass, on gravel, in the sun"
"To spend uncounted years of pain"
In a Gondola ("Afloat we move; delicious! ah") [from *Dipsychus*, Scene IV, 1–34]
"O let me love my love unto myself alone" [*Dipsychus*, Scene IV, 82–101, but in the
    earlier version printed in *Poems* 538–539]

1865 Letters and Remains of Arthur Hugh Clough, (For Private Circulation Only)
        (London 1865)   *86*

This volume, apparently edited by Mrs Clough in consultation with others, includes the
following poems here printed for the first time:

"Truth is a golden thread"
"Whence com'st thou, shady lane"
"So I as boyish years went by, went wrong"
Easter Day. Naples, 1849

Easter Day. II
Dipsychus
Dipsychus Continued. A Fragment

For comment on some of the textual problems raised by *Dipsychus,* see *Poems* 528–530; and see R. Gollin, "The 1951 Edition of Clough's *Poems,*" *MP* LX (November 1962) 125–127. Mrs Clough was, as she said, "afraid on the whole that I shall not have courage to publish it," not only because she regarded it as "too unfinished," but even more because she feared for the impression it would give of Clough's religious beliefs. In *Poems,* p 529, the editors print part of her letter to the Rev Percival Graves stressing the first point; the unprinted part stresses the second (see MS d 139, No 1156 in *C* II 646). In it, she wonders "what Mr. Jowett would say" of her publishing the whole poem, since "he was formerly against giving more than extracts"; and she asks Graves to suggest "passages you think deserving of being extracted." She then writes:

"I believe, to go back to what you say of the general tendency of the poem, that the end is left indistinct because it was so in his own mind. I cannot think he meant the feeling of religion in one sort or other to succumb but that he did think there must be a time of dearth so to speak in a practical life, especially to a mind somewhat overfed in youth. I [regret?] so much that he did not live to do more, because I think he would have done differently later. He did change enough to make me think he would have gone farther and this also makes me shrink from giving out anything which might *look* as if it was the final result at which he had attained." Mrs Clough ended by printing a bowdlerized version.

In this edition Mrs Clough also prints *Dipsychus Continued: a Fragment,* calling it "a sketch for a continuation of 'Dipsychus,' written much later" and "in no sense a second part" (p 146). In her letter to Graves she stresses her belief that this addendum to the poem is not, properly speaking, a progressive development from it: "I think the continuation 30 years after, tho most unsatisfactory, was a sort of citing of common place views as having a degree of truth in them."

1869 *The Poems and Prose Remains of Arthur Hugh Clough, with a Selection from His Letters,* edited by his wife (2 vols, London 1869), with a memoir by Mrs Clough   87

For the memoir see Part III, No 112. Vol II, containing the poems, is the source of nearly all subsequent editions. It was edited with "the valuable assistance . . . in making these selections and in arranging these volumes" of John Addington Symonds (Preface to Vol I); Mrs Clough acknowledged as well that his "taste and judgment" was operative throughout. Possibly Symonds manifested his taste in two additional ways: nearly all of the previously untitled poems are here provided with titles, usually with no authority from the MSS; and all of the shorter poems are divided into eight groups, each group provided with a title. The texts, as the editors of *Poems* note, p 475, are not reliable, but the edition adds more than half again as many poems as had been previously published posthumously. *We have marked these new poems with an asterisk* *.

EARLY POEMS

Thoughts of Home ("I watched them from the window," from the *RM,* No 43 above) *
An Evening Walk in Spring ("It was but some few nights ago," from the *RM,* No 49 above) *
An Incident ("'Twas on a sunny summer day," from the *RM,* No 52 above) *
The Thread of Truth ("Truth is a golden thread, seen here and there")
Revival ("So I went wrong")
The Shady Lane ("Whence comest thou? shady lane, and why and how?")
The Higher Courage ("Come back again, my olden heart!")
Written on a Bridge ("When soft September brings again")
A River Pool ("Sweet streamlet bason! at thy side")
In a Lecture-Room ("Away, haunt thou not me")
'Blank Misgivings of a Creature moving about in Worlds not realized' (including I and IV, but X still printed separately below)
A Song of Autumn ("My wind is turned to bitter north")
τὸ καλόν ("I have seen higher holier things than these")
Χρυσέα κλὴς ἐπὶ γλώσσα ("If, when in cheerless wanderings, dull and cold")
The Silver Wedding

The Music of the World and of the Soul
    I   "Why should I say I see the things I see not?" *
    II "Are there not, then, two musics unto men?"
    III "Yea, and as thought of some departed friend"
Love, not Duty ("Thought may well be ever ranging")
Love and Reason ("Where panting sighs the bosom fill")
ὁ Θεὸς μετὰ σοῦ ("Farewell, my Highland lassie!")
Wirkung in der Ferne ("When the dews are earliest falling")
ἐπὶ Λάτμῳ ("On the mountain, in the woodland") *
A Protest ("Light words they were, and lightly, falsely said")
Sic Itur
Parting ("O tell me, friends, while yet we part")
Qua Cursum Ventus
'Wen Gott betrügt, ist wohl betrogen' ("Is it true, ye gods, who treat us") *

POEMS ON RELIGIOUS AND BIBLICAL SUBJECTS

Fragments of the Mystery of the Fall (i.e. *Adam and Eve*)*
The Song of Lamech
Genesis XXIV *
Jacob
Jacob's Wives *
The New Sinai ("Lo, here is God, and there is God!")
Qui laborat, orat
ὕμνος ἄυμνος ("O Thou whose image in the shrine")
The Hidden Love ("O let me love my love unto myself alone") [*Dipsychus*, Scene IV, 82–
    101, but in the earlier version printed in *Poems*, p 538–539]
Shadow and Light ("Cease, empty Faith, the Spectrum saith")
'With Whom is no Variableness, neither Shadow of Turning' ("It fortifies my soul to know")
In Stratis Viarum ("Blessed are those who have not seen")
'Perchè pensa? Pensando s'invecchia' ("To spend uncounted years of pain")
'O thou of little Faith' ("It may be true") *
'Through a Glass darkly' ("What we, when face to face we see")
Ah! yet consider it again ("Old things need not be therefore true")
Noli æmulari ("In controversial foul impureness") *
'What went ye out for to see?' ("Across the sea, along the shore")
Epi-strauss-ium *
The Shadow (*a Fragment*) ("I dreamed a dream") *
Easter Day (Naples 1849)
Easter Day, II

DIPSYCHUS

Prologue
Part I
Part II
Epilogue

DIPSYCHUS CONTINUED (*a Fragment*)

POEMS ON LIFE AND DUTY

Duty ("Duty — that's to say, complying")
Life is Struggle ("To wear out heart, and nerves, and brain") *
In the Great Metropolis
The Latest Decalogue
The Questioning Spirit ("The human spirits saw I on a day")
Bethesda (a Sequel)
Hope evermore and believe!
Blessed are they who have not seen! ("O happy they whose hearts receive") *
Cold Comfort ("Say, will it, when our hairs are grey") *
Sehnsucht ("Whence are ye, vague desires")
High and Low ("The grasses green of sweet content") *

All is well ("Whate'er you dream with doubt possest") *
πάντα ῥεῖ — οὐδὲν μένει ("Upon the water, in the boat")
The Stream of Life ("O stream descending to the sea")
In a London Square ("Put forth thy leaf, thou lofty plane")

THE BOTHIE OF TOBER-NA-VUOLICH: *a Long-Vacation Pastoral*

IDYLLIC SKETCHES

Ite Domum Saturae, venit Hesperus ("The skies have sunk, and hid the upper snow")
A London Idyll ("On grass, on gravel, in the sun")
Natura naturans *

AMOURS DE VOYAGE

SEVEN SONNETS ON THE THOUGHT OF DEATH (With a footnote stating that they
have been "brought together from very imperfect MSS") *

MARI MAGNO OR TALES ON BOARD *

The Lawyer's First Tale: Primitiae or Third Cousins
The Clergyman's First Tale: Love is Fellow-Service
My Tale: A la banquette, or a Modern Pilgrimage
The Mate's Story
The Clergyman's Second Tale
The Lawyer's Second Tale: Christian

SONGS IN ABSENCE (consisting of the following untitled poems)

"Farewell, Farewell! Her vans the vessel tries" *
"Ye flags of Piccadilly" *
"Come home, come home!"
"Green fields of England!"
"Come back, come back,"
"Some future day when what is now is not"
"Where lies the land to which the ship would go?"
"The mighty ocean rolls and raves"
"That out of sight is out of mind"
"Were you with me, or I with you"
"Am I with you, or you with me?" *
"Were I with you, or you with me" *
"Were you with me, or I with you *
"O ship, ship, ship" *

ESSAYS IN CLASSICAL METRES

Translations of Iliad * [in *Poems* 451–454]
Elegiacs ("From thy far sources") * ("Trunks the forest yielded")
Alcaics ("So spake the voice")
Actaeon *

MISCELLANEOUS POEMS

Come, Poet, come!
The Dream Land ("To think that men of former days") *
In the Depths ("It is not sweet content, be sure")
Darkness (*a Fragment*) ("But that from slow dissolving pomps of dawn") *
Two Moods ("Ah, blame him not because he's gay!") *
Youth and Age ("Dance on, dance on, we see, we see")
Solvitur acris Hiems *
Thesis and Antithesis *
ἀνεμώλια ("Go, foolish thoughts, and join the throng") *
Columbus ("How in God's name did Columbus get over")
Even the Winds and the Sea obey *
Repose in Egypt *

To a Sleeping Child ("Lips, lips, open!")
Translations from Goethe *
Uranus *
Selene *
At Rome ("O, richly soiled and richly sunned") *
Last Words. Napoleon and Wellington. *
Peschiera
Alteram Partem
Say not the struggle nought availeth

1871–85   Nine Reissued Versions of 1869   88

Between 1869 and 1951 Clough's poems were reissued many times, though with only one significant attempt to establish more accurate texts (No 94) prior to 1951. Clough's popular appeal during the last decades of the nineteenth century and the first decade of the twentieth led publishers to imply or state that their reprints were new editions; this created several related families of reprintings, each of which is given a separate listing in this catalogue.

The publishers apparently called 1862 (No 83) the "First Edition," 1863 (No 85) the "Second Edition," and an 1871 reprinting of 1869 the "Third Edition" — perhaps to discriminate the separate volumes of poetry from those volumes being issued in conjunction with *Prose Remains*. This "Third Edition," which contained an abridged form of Mrs Clough's memoir printed in 1869, was then reissued in 1874, 1877, 1878, 1879, 1880, and 1882. A "Fourth Edition," identical to the "Third," was issued in 1883 and reprinted in 1885.

1884 *The Bothie, and Other Poems.* Edited by Ernest Rhys (London and New York, n. d.). Reissued in 1896   89

The "other poems" are the *Ambarvalia* poems (No 72) except for "Look you, my simple friend, 'tis one of those"; and in addition two poems from the first "Letter of Parepidemus" (see Part II No 61), namely "Upon the water in a boat" and "In vain I seem to call." Some of these poems are haphazardly retitled: e.g. "Away, haunt not thou me" is called *Vain Philosophy*.

1888 *Qua Cursum Ventus* (Boston 1888)   90

—— Seven Reissued Versions of 1869 called *Poems of Arthur Hugh Clough,* New and Revised Edition (London 1888)   91

Called hereafter the "Fifth Edition," and calling itself a "New Edition, with Additions," the table of contents and texts of this edition show it identical to 1869 in all but one respect: it eliminates *Thoughts of Home* from the section called EARLY POEMS. There is no memoir, and no editor is named. Reprinted in 1890, 1892, 1895, 1898, 1903, and 1909; and see Nos 95 and 97.

1894 *Selections from the Poems of Arthur Hugh Clough* (Golden Treasury Series, London, 1894). Reprinted 1894 (again), 1904, and 1909   92

The Preface, p v–vi, is signed B.M.S.C. (i.e., Mrs Clough), which suggests that the selection and notes may also be hers.

THE BOTHIE OF TOBER-NA-VUOLICH

EARLY POEMS:

Revival ("So I went wrong")
In a Lecture-Room ("Away, haunt thou not me")
A Song of Autumn ("My wind is turned to bitter north")
τὸ καλόν ("I have seen higher, holier things than these")
Χρυσέα κλης ἐπὶ γλώσσα ("If, when in cheerless wanderings, dull and cold")
The Music of the World and of the Soul ("Why should I say I see the things I see not")
Qua Cursum Ventus

'Wen Gott Betrügt, ist Wohl Betrogen' ("Is it true, ye gods, Who treat us")
The New Sinai ("Lo, here is God, and there is God!")
The Questioning Spirit ("The human spirits saw I on a day")
Bethesda. A Sequel
Qui Laborat, Orat

FROM DIPSYCHUS

The Piazza at Night [*Poems*, Scene X, 1–126, 140–141)]
" 'There is no God,' the wicked saith" [*Poems*, Scene V, 154–185]
In a Gondola [*Poems*, Scene IV, 3–34, 236–257, and an ealier draft of 296–305]
"The world is very odd we see" [*Poems*, Scene IV, 114–121]
"O let me love my love unto myself alone" [*Poems*, IV, 82–101]
"Where are the great, whom thou would'st wish to praise thee?" [*Poems*, Scene IV, 122–127]
Spectator ab extra [*Poems*, Scene IV, 130–195]
"Submit, submit!" [*Poems*, Scene IX, 160–181, Scene X, 163–170, and Scene XI, 87–104, 202–213]
"When the enemy is near thee" [*Poems*, XII, 8–31]

FROM AMOURS DE VOYAGE

[*Poems*, Canto I, 1–32, 152–201; Canto II, 252–283; Canto III, 107–150, 214–239; Canto V, 118–124, 181–185; Canto III, 293–304]

MISCELLANEOUS POEMS

'With whom is no Variableness, neither Shadow of Turning' ("It fortifies my soul to know")
The Latest Decalogue
Hope Evermore and Believe
'Through a Glass Darkly' ("What we, when face to face we see")
Ah! yet consider it again! ("Old things need not be therefore true")
'Ite Domum Saturae, Venit Hesperus' ("The skies have sunk and hid the upper snow")
A London Idyll ("On grass, on gravel, in the sun")
The Stream of Life ("O stream descending to the sea")
In a London Square ("Put forth thy leaf, thou lofty plane")
The Shadow ("I dreamed a dream")
Easter Day. Naples, 1849
Easter Day. II
Peschiera
Say not the Struggle nought availeth
Songs written on ship-board ("Farewell, farewell," "Come home, come home"; "Green fields of England"; "Come back, come back"; "Some future day"; "Where lies the land")
Come, Poet, Come!

[*1906*] *The Poetical Works of Arthur Hugh Clough* (London, The Muses' Library, n. d.), with a memoir by F. T. Palgrave   **93**

Identical to the British 1862 edition, giving the same poems in the same order, but using alphabetical order in its table of contents.

1910 Poems of Clough, including "Ambarvalia," both versions of "The Bothie," "Amours de Voyage," etc., edited by H. S. Milford (London 1910)   **94**

For the prefatory essay by Milford see Part III, No 240
This edition carefully re-edits the British 1862 edition, collating it with the 1849 *Ambarvalia* and a copy of the 1848 *Bothie* corrected by Clough himself. Variant readings and additional lines are given in footnotes. It groups together and reprints all of the original *Ambarvalia* poems, and so reprints the following for the first time:

"Ah, what is love, our love, she said"
"I give thee joy! O worthy word!"

Commemoration Sonnets (all three)
"Oh, ask not what is love, she said"
"With graceful seat and skilful hand"
"Look you, my simple friend, 'tis one of those"

Also for the first time since the original publication of *Ambarvalia*, it prints "I have seen higher holier things than these" as the tenth and final poem of the series called *'Blank Misgivings.'* This edition is neither informed nor misinformed by the editions of 1862, 1862 (American), 1863, 1865, or 1869; it prints none of the additional poems given in those editions, but neither does it print the unauthorized titles of 1869 *et seq.*

1911 Poems of Arthur Hugh Clough (New York, n. d.)   **95**

Identical with the 1869 edition (No 87), including Mrs Clough's "Memoir," but like the 1888 edition (No 91) omitting "Thoughts of Home."
Thomas Y. Crowell Co, the publisher, has kindly informed us of the date.

1912 Poems (Oxford, n. d.) [Half title: Oxford Plain Texts]   Reissued 1914   **96**

Qua cursum ventus
Written on a bridge ("When soft September brings again")
The stream of Life ("O stream, descending to the sea")
On a London Square ("Put forth thy leaf, thou lofty plane")
Ite Domum saturae, venit Hesperus ("The skies have sunk and hid the upper snow")
Peschiera
Alteram Partem
"Say not, the struggle nought availeth"
"Come home, come home, and where is home for me"
"Come back, come back, behold with straining mast"
"Some future day, when what is now is not"
"Where lies the land to which the ship would go?"
"Were you with me, or I with you"
Spectator ab extra [*Dipsychus*, Scene IV, 130–141, 190–195]
The Latest Decalogue
'There is no god,' the wicked saith [*Dipsychus*, Scene V, 154–185]
Extracts from *The Bothie of Tober-na-vuolich* [in *Poems*, Canto I, 1–81, 121–179; III, 19–
    67; II, 124–130; V, 9–29; VI, 1–30; IX, 109–137, 192–200]
Extracts from *Amours de Voyage* [In *Poems*, Canto I, 186–201; III, 214–239; III, 1–16;
    II, 97–146; V, 214–224]

1913 Poems of Arthur Hugh Clough, with an introduction by Charles Whibley
        (London 1913)   **97**

For the introduction see Part III, No 255.
The table of contents is identical with that of the 1888 edition (No 91), and thus also with No 95. Reprinted in 1920.

1919 Gaisford Greek Verse, 1919. From A. H. Clough's "Amours de Voyage"
        (Oxford 1919)   **98**

"All the Elegiacs in the first three Cantos" are printed parallel to a translation of them into Greek by G. R. Driver.

1951 The Poems of Arthur Hugh Clough, edited by H. F. Lowry, A. L. P. Norring-
        ton, and F. L. Mulhauser, with a prefatory essay by A. L. P. Norrington
        (Oxford 1951)   **99**

For the essay, see Part III, No 372.

This valuable but flawed work is now the standard edition. The editors returned to the original manuscripts for their texts, provided textual notes and — also in the notes — provided many variant, cancelled, and additional lines. They eliminated titles posthumously given the poems (eliminating as well, unfortunately, some titles given on Clough's authority), added approximately six hundred lines to previously published poems, and printed for the first time the following new poems:

"Enough, small Room; tho' all too true" (p 47)
To the Great Metropolis (p 48)
"Would that I were, — O hear thy suppliant, thou" (p 49)
Sa Majesté Très Chrétienne (p 69)
"These vulgar ways that round me be" (p 74)
July's Farewell (p 75)
Chorus (p 77)
O Qui Me (p 106)
"If to write, rewrite, and write again" (p 435)
Epithalamium (p 445)
Prologue for *Box and Cox* (p 450; actually, an Epilogue — see *C* II 337)

They also printed for the first time *The American's Tale* (subtitled "Juxtaposition") in the text of *Mari Magno* (p 342); and they reprinted for the first time two *RM* poems (Nos 47 and 58 above). Unfortunately, they omitted a great many poems, lines, and fragments, among them the complete or incomplete unpublished poems listed above, and the new previously published poems listed above. For an account of other flaws in this edition see R. Gollin, "The 1951 Edition of Clough's *Poems*: a Critical Reexamination," *MP* LX (November 1962) 120–127.

Part II: Prose[1]

CLOUGH'S PROSE, which is of great importance for the study of his poetry and of Victorian social and literary criticism, has been curiously neglected. The small attention scholars have given to it has not been perceptive; and until recently the only available texts have been woefully inadequate. The *Prose Remains* were published by Mrs Clough with the poetry in 1869, and separately in 1888. Both editions printed only extracts from three of the essays, deleted without warning or explanation a number of paragraphs of Clough's final texts, from the other eight,[2] and omitted six lectures called "Dryden and His Times," four on Jonathan Swift, one apiece on language, classical metres, William Cowper, and Walter Scott, the two prefaces to Plutarch, and a review of translations from Goethe, not to mention all of Clough's early work at Rugby, eight letters to magazines, and a large number of fragments and unfinished essays in manuscript. At long last, in 1964, Buckner Trawick's *Selected Prose Works* made amends by printing a sizable amount of Clough's work. But there is still no complete edition.[3]

The following list includes, we hope, everything known to exist, in print or manuscript, which could be called a "prose work." Only personal letters, journals, and jottings in notebooks have been excluded. In an Appendix, evidence for the possible existence of other items is added. So far as the dates can be determined, the order is chronological; the date given is that of composition when known, otherwise that of first publication.

The first items (Nos 1–13) comprise Clough's prose contributions to the *Rugby Magazine*. Clough was an editor from the beginning and sole editor after the second issue (cf *C* I 22–23). His articles are signed T. Y. C. ("Thos Yankee Clough" or "Two Years Old Colt": *C* I 32), Z (*C* I 28) or A.V. (see No 7). In various dialogues among the editors Clough is called

---

[1] This section is a revised and expanded version of Walter E. Houghton's "The Prose Works of Arthur Hugh Clough: A Checklist and Calendar, with Some Unpublished Passages" *Bulletin of the New York Public Library* LXIV (July 1960) 377–394 and the "Supplementary List" LXXI (Jan 1967) 55–58.

[2] There are only ten items, however, in the 1888 edition because the review of F. W. Newman's *The Soul* (No 36) was not reprinted. In both editions we count the "Letters of Parepidemus" as two items, viz, Nos 61 and 62.

[3] For bibliographical description of the three editions, see below, Nos 74–76. In the following pages they are cited, respectively, as *PPR*, *PR*, and *SPW*.

Clayton. There is an "Alphabetical Index" of titles and authors (by initials) in Vol II 407–412. On this magazine, also see the note preceding No 38 in Part I.

The short introductions that Clough wrote for sets of poems — his own and those of others — have not been listed. They may be found in Vol I 172–173, 398–399; and in II 388–389, 391–392, 393–394. The two prefaces, for the first and second issues, placed at the start of Vol I in the Vassar College copy. are unsigned, but may well have been written by Clough.

1835 July   "Introductory" I 9–14, signed T. Y. C.   *1*
An apologia for a school magazine.

——— ———   "Ten Minutes before Locking-up" I 91–95, indexed T. Y. C.   *2*
This schoolboy conversation in a humorous vein is claimed by Clough (*C* I 32).

——— *October*   "Macaulay's 'Battle of Ivry'" I 123–132, signed T. Y. C.   *3*
Reprinted in *SPW* 29–38.
This essay on poetry, stressing the distinctions between subjective and objective art, is much indebted to Coleridge. Cf *C* I 73–74, 76–78 (by J. P. Gell), and 83.

——— ———   "October" I 199–205, signed T. Y. C.   *4*
This dialogue of the editors is claimed by Clough, *C* I 19.

1836 January   "School Society" I 207–215, indexed T. Y. C.   *5*
A study of school friendships, their value and their moral dangers.

——— *April*   "A Long Talk" I 311–319, signed T. Y. C.   *6*
Reprinted in *SPW* 39–47.
A dialogue on Wordsworth's *Excursion*, Books I and II, and on poetry in general.

——— *July*   "Henry Sinclair or, 'Tis Six Years Ago'" II 56–61, signed A. V., indexed T. Y. C.   *7*
Reprinted in *CPW* 297–302.
If "Henry Sinclair" is not fictitious, the name is probably a pseudonym.

——— ———   "May it please your Royal Majesty" II 103–104, signed "The Scholars of Rugby School," indexed T. Y. C.   *8*
A mock invitation to William IV to visit the school. In the "Alphabetical Index" it is called "Letter to the King."

——— *December*   "The Rugby Register" II 105–111, signed T. Y. C.   *9*
Review of *The Rugby Register from the Year 1675 to the Present Time* (Rugby 1836), a local history of the school and the town. The article focusses on the moral or immoral character of different types of boys.

1837 July   "A Peripateticographical Article" II 223–234   *10*
This description of the Rugby countryside with illustrative poems is assigned to "T. Y. C. &c." in the "Alphabetical Index." Clough probably planned the article and wrote the prose. For the poems, see above Part I, No 53.

——— ———   "Sonnets in the Abstract" II 270–274, indexed T. Y. C.   *11*
Reprinted in *SPW* 48–52.
This discussion of the sonnet as a poetic form emphasizes what kinds of experience it is well fitted or poorly fitted to embody.

—— *November*   "Two Autumn Days in Athens" II 348–358, signed T. Y. C.   **12**

A combination of three scenes imitating Greek drama with a fourth scene of historical description. The subject is an incident in the Peloponnesian War. Clough's footnote to the title reads: "B.C. 429, early in October. Thucydides, II, 93, 94. Thirlwall's Greece, Vol. III, pp. 157 and 166."

—— ——   "Address of Leave-taking" II 398–400   **13**

A general farewell on the termination of the magazine.
There is no such title in the "Alphabetical Index," but I assume that the Address is there called "Breaking Up," a title assigned to T. Y. C. but not found elsewhere in either volume.

1837–38   Undergraduate essays   **14**

Fourteen essays, each initialed by a tutor, in a notebook (Bodleian MSS) called "English Essays," and marked at the top corner, "Balliol College, October 1837." They were written between that date and February or March 1839 (see the date of no XIII). The titles are as follows:

I   On the Effect of Dramatic Representations on the Taste and Morals of a People
   Reprinted in *SPW* 53–56.

II   On some of the principal Effects on Literature resulting from the Invention of Printing

III   Venice

IV   What is the reason that the Law of Nations has been more studied by the Moderns, than by the Ancients?

V   Usque adeo magni refert studium atque voluptas,
   Et quibus in rebus consuerint esse operati,
   Non homines solum, sed vero animalia cuncta.
                                                                — Lucretius [4]

VI   *May 5th*   Ego autem satis mirari non queo, unde hoc sit tam insolens domesticarum rerum fastidium.
                                                                — Cic. de Fin. I.3 [5]

VII   Examine the truth of νέων δὲ πάντες οἱ μεγάλοι καὶ οἱ πολλοὶ πόνοι.[6]

VIII   On the advantages and disadvantages of Contemporary History

IX   Etenim nescio quo pacto magis in studio homines timor quam fiducia decet.
                                                                — Pliny.[7]

X   *Nov 23*   The Influence of the Progress of Luxury & Refinement on Literature
   Reprinted in *SPW* 57–59.

XI   The History and Influence of the Stoical Philosophy

XII   The Philosophy of History

XIII   *Feb 8th*   The Prevalence under different circumstances of different Systems of Philosophy considered as an index of the Character of any Age or Nation

XIV   Examine how far Aristotle's View of the Virtues in his 4th Book of Ethics is deficient

[4] *De Rerum Natura*, IV.984–986, where the activity of imagination is being discussed. Paraphrased by Clough: "So important is it what habits have been cultivated, what faculties called into employment, not only in the case of men, but also in all animals whatever."

[5] *De Finibus* I.iii.10, translated by H. Rackham (Loeb Library): "But for my part I can never cease wondering what can be the origin of the exaggerated contempt for home products that is now fashionable." Cicero is speaking about the Romans' aversion to the Latin language and literature.

[6] Plato *Republic* VII.536d, translated by Clough: "The Young have for their share all the greatest & heaviest labours of human life."

[7] Pliny the Younger, somewhere in the *Epistolae*: "For I do not know why in learning mistrust becomes men more than confidence."

1839–40　Undergraduate essays　　　　　　　　　　　　　　　**15**

　　　　Fourteen essays in a similar notebook (Bodleian MSS) called "English Essays, Balliol College, April, 1839." They were written between that date and May 1840. The titles are as follows:

I　*April 19 1830*　The Poetical Character of Sophocles
　　Reprinted in *SPW* 60–62.

II　The Social Condition of the Greeks & the State of Moral Feeling prevalent among them illustrated by the Events of the Peloponnesian War

III　Περὶ δε τῆς πρὸς τὴν θάλατταν κοινωνίας πότερον ὠφέλιμος ταῖς πόλεοιν ἡ βλαβέρα, πολλὰ τυγχάνουσιν ἀμφισβητοῦντες [8]
　　Reprinted in *SPW* 205–207.

IV　Τέχνη τύχην ἔστερξε καὶ τύχη τέχνην.[9] The Influence on the Progress of Civilisation exerted by Causes beyond human Control

V　*October 18th 1839*　On the differences of the Religious Systems of Greece & Rome

VI　*November 1st*　The Protection afforded to the Person & Property of a Roman Citizen by the Judicial Tribunals of the Republic

VII　The Moral Effect of Works of Satire
　　Reprinted in *SPW* 63–65.

VIII　From an Examination of the first Book of Aristotle's Politics point out the imperfect View of Society taken by the Wisest of the Greeks

IX　*February 1st 1840*　Τῶ ὑπερβάλλοντι φθονοῦντες ἤδη καὶ ἀπιστοῦσιν [10]

X　Ὁ δὲ μὴ δυνάμενος κοινωνεῖν ἢ μηθὲν δεόμενος δι' ἀντάρκεισν οὐδὲν μέρος πόλεως, ὥστε θηρίον ἢ θεός. Arist. Polit. 1 [11]

XI　*Feb 29th*　On the System of Education pursued at Athens under Pericles

XII　*March 27th*　A Comparison of the Effects of Conquest & of Commerce on Civilisation

XIII　*May 16th*　Capessentibus rem publicam nihilo minus quam philosophis adhibenda est magnificentia et rerum humanarum despicientia.
　　　　　　　　　　　　　　　　　　　　　　　　　— Cic. de Off. 1.21 [12]

XIV　*May 30th*　Ἀνδρῶν ἐπιφανῶν πᾶσα γῆ τάφος [13]

1840–41　Undergraduate essays　　　　　　　　　　　　　　**16**

　　　　Six essays in a similar notebook (Bodleian MSS) called, "English Essays, October, 1840." They were written between that date and February 1841. The titles are as follows:

[8] "People differ greatly about whether foreign trade is beneficial or harmful to well governed cities."

[9] Line from a lost play by Agathon quoted by Aristotle in the *Nicomachean Ethics* VI.iv.–1140a.20, translated by Clough: "'Art helpeth Fortune, Fortune Art' (if we regard Art as significant of all that is, and Fortune of all that is not, dependent upon human Will for its origination."

[10] Thucydides II.35.2, from Pericles' funeral oration. Clough's translation of this difficult sentence is: "What is beyond them they from envy at once disbelieve."

[11] Aristotle *Politics* I.1.12, translated by H. Rackham (Loeb Library): "But he who is unable to live in society, or who is so self-sufficient that he has no need to do so, is no part of a state, so that he must be either a beast or a god."

[12] *De Officiis* I.xxi.72, translated by Walter Miller (Loeb Library): "Statesmen, no less than philosophers, should carry with them greatness of spirit and indifference to outward circumstances."

[13] Thucydides II.43.3, from Pericles' funeral oration: "Famous men have the whole earth for memorial."

1841–42?   Addenda ad Apocalypsin secundum interpretationem vulgatam   **17**

This facetious dialogue of 5½ pages [14] in Latin between Spiritus and Pandemia (the flesh) appears in a notebook marked "Latin Prose" by Mrs Clough, now at the Bodleian Library. Both the nature of the dialogue and the lack of any tutor's initials indicate that it was not an undergraduate exercise.[15] It was probably written not long after Clough passed his examination in April 1841.

The subject and tone anticipate the dialogue in the opening scenes of *Dipsychus*, which shows — if the date is correct — that about the time Clough took his degree, he was moving out from the shadow of Dr Arnold's moral rigor. Pandemia is the "common" or "vulgar" Aphrodite (Eros pandemos), who is contrasted with the "heavenly" Aphrodite in a passage in Plato's "Symposium," 180–181, which Clough must have had in mind. His Latin title, therefore, in which "vulgatam" is a pun, seems to mean: "A further and quite unspiritual revelation according to the vulgar — not the Vulgate — interpretation." (The last syllable of "Apocalypsin" is a trans-literation of the Greek.)

1842–46   Seventy-seven biographies contributed to *Dictionary of Greek and Roman Biography and Myth*, ed William Smith (3 vols, London 1844–1849), each signed A. H. C.   **18**

Clough's articles are in vol ɪ 19 (Admetus), 69 (Ageselaus I), 69–70 (Agesilaus II), 96 (Alcamenes), 163 (Anaxander, Anaxandra, Anaxandrides), 164 (Anaxidamus), 205 (Antiphemus), 260 (Archedice), 264 (Archelaus), 265 (Archias), 266 (Archidamus I), 266–267 (Archidamus II), 280 (Argileonis), 289 (Aristagoras), 293–294 (Aristeides), 297 (Aristeus), 304 (Aristodemus), 309 (Ariston, Ariston), 349–350 (Arrhibaeus), 369–370 (Artas), 386 (Asopius), 390–391 (Astyochus), 402 (Athenagoras), 502–503 (Brasidas), 679 (Chalcideus), 689 (Charminus, Charoeades), 749–751 (Cimon), 779 (Cleandridas), 781 (Clearidas), 790 (Cleobulus), 791 (Cleombrotus), 797–798 (Cleon), 911 (Cynane), 958–959 (Demaratus), 979–981 (Demosthenes), 994 (Derdas), 1009 (Diitrephes), 1018 (Diodotus), 1026–1027 (Diomedon), 1027 (Diomilus), 1055 (Diotrephes, Diphilus), 1066–1067 (Dorieus), 1067 (Dorieus); and in vol ɪɪ 3 (Echestratus), 16 (Endius), 60 (Evarchus), 75 (Eucrates), 95 (Eunomus), 97 (Euphemus), 102–103 (Eupompidas), 109 (Eurycrates), 110 (Eurylochus), 111 (Eurymachus), 111–112 (Eurymedon), 112 (Eurypon), 113 (Eurysthenes), 123–124 (Euthydemus), 279 (Gongylus), 324–325 (Hagnon), 367 (Hegesandridas), 423 (Hermon), 480 (Hippocles, Hippoclus), 572 (Inaros), 699 (Lacadaemonius), 701 (Laco), 709 (Laespedias), 713 (Lamachus), 726–727 6(Leagrus), 734 (Leo), 750 (Leocrates), 866 (Lysicles).

The life of "Agesilaus," written in Nov 1842, seems to have been the first of the series: cf *C* ɪ 122. Clough was busy at work on the lives in June and July 1844: cf *C* ɪ 127, 131. Since he did not contribute to vol ɪɪɪ, we adopt the publication year of vol ɪɪ as the terminal date for this item.

1843 February 2   Latin speech delivered at Oriel College on the occasion of his reception as a Fellow   **19**

In MS in the Oriel College Library. Cf *C* ɪɪ 371.

[14] Here and throughout this section of the *Bibliography* the word "pages" applied to a MS means pages of text, excluding pages that are blank.

[15] After the title some one has written, "Check HFL," the initials of the Clough scholar, Howard Foster Lowry.

1844 "Illustrations of Latin Lyrical Metres" *The Classical Museum, a Journal of Philology, and of Ancient History and Literature* IV (1847) 347–363, signed A. H. Clough   **20**

An essay on the metrics of translation, with illustrations taken largely from Horace. *C* I 142, shows that much, if not all of it, was written by Dec 31 1844. It is described, with verse quotations, by Geoffrey Tillotson. *Times Literary Supplement* (June 18 1954) 400. (See Part I, Nos 67–69.)

1846 January 23 Letter to the Editor *The Balance* p 26, signed M. A. O.   **21**

Reprinted in *SPA* 208–210, where the editor has entitled it "The Repeal of the Corn-laws."

An interpolation in the original text, properly omitted in *SPW*, but printed there in the notes, p 342, was part of the previous letter signed "R" and should have gone at the bottom of the last column overleaf, not at the bottom of the first column on p 26.[16]

For the attribution to Clough of this and the next five letters, see *C* I 167, 168, 169. The initials probably stand for "Master of Arts, Oxon."

The letters were written under the marked influence of Carlyle, in particular of *Past and Present*. Except for No 24 they all deal with the proper attitude of the rich toward society and especially toward the working class. Much of the material in Clough's tract on *Retrenchment* (No 29 below) was first developed in Nos 23 and 24.

—— *January 30* "Political Economy" *The Balance* p 34, signed M. A. O.   **22**

Reprinted in *SPW* 211–213.

—— *February 6* "The Militia" *The Balance* p 42, signed M. A. O.   **23**

Reprinted in *SPW* 214–216.

This is a reply to some moral problems about serving in a militia, problems raised by "J.M.F." in a letter immediately following Clough's letter of Jan 30. With characteristic two-sidedness, Clough explores the pros and cons of the use of force.

—— *February 13* "Expensive Living" *The Balance* p 50, signed M. A. O.   **24**

Reprinted in *SPW* 217–221.
Cf *C* I 168, 169.

—— *March 6* "A Few Practical Hints" *The Balance* p 77, signed M. A. O.   **25**

Reprinted in *SPW* 221–223.

—— *March 20* "The Spirit of Trade" *The Balance* p 93–94, signed M. A. O.   **26**

Reprinted in *SPW* 223–225.

1846–1847? Paper on Expenditure   **27**

This Bodleian MS of 20 pages is an attack on unnecessary consumption and on the defense of luxuries because they provide employment: of Nos 22, 24, 29, 30. Professor Evelyn Barish of Cornell, in a letter to the editors, pointed out that the reference to Cobden's continental tour being a natural benefit to England dates the paper between Aug 5 1846 and Oct 11 1847.

1846 Autumn Conversations between the Sun and the Moon   **28**

This Bodleian MS containing 38 pages consists of short fables illustrating, in part at least, the different way things look from different positions. The reference to Neptune having "just" been found out suggests the above date, since the planet was first discovered in September 1846. Miss Barish (see previous item) argues for a date of c December 1851 – January 1852 "because the paper is identical to some Clough used in letters during these months and never,

[16] For the analysis of this confusion we are indebted to Mr Robindra Biswas of York University, Toronto.

so far as I can tell, before or later"; and thinks the discovery of Neptune such a remarkable and unique event that for some years it could have been said to have "just" occurred.

1847 May   A Consideration of Objections against the Retrenchment Association (Oxford 1847)   29

This tract, written in reply to the objections raised against the Association in the *Oxonian* for May, was reprinted in *PPR* I 273–290 and in *PR* 283–301 as "A Consideration of Objections against the Retrenchment Association at Oxford during the Irish Famine in 1847"; and in *SPW* 226–240 under the published title. Although Mrs Clough apparently planned to reprint only "the substance" (*PPR* I 109 or *PR* 111), she gave the whole text almost verbatim.

For comments by Clough, see *C* I 301 and Mrs Clough's letter to C. E. Norton, May 5 1862 (Harvard MSS), where she reports that Clough thought it "not fair towards the New-manish party, whose especial characteristic it was to practice both self-denial and charity in an extreme degree." For Emerson's reaction in 1847, see *C* I 186n, 187. Bonamy Price's conserva-tive objections are in a long, unpublished letter to Clough of May 30 1847, in the Bodleian Library. There is a digest and commentary by Godfrey Lushington in *Letters and Remains of Arthur Hugh Clough* (London 1865) 92–99. George David Boyle, *Recollections* (London 1895) 124–125, reported that it "had an effect of a certain kind, in moderating expenses and making some people save money in the midst of their dissipations in a summer term."

1847?   Letter on the Rights of Property   30

Reprinted in *SPW* 241–242.

This brief, incomplete MS (Bodleian), which starts "My dear Sir," was written at Oxford ("I see around me greedy, luxurious, and apathetic gentleman-commoners"), and was almost certainly a reply to Price's letter of May 30 1847 (see previous item). It begins: "I am pretty sure that I agree with all you say on the Rights of Property — and I incline to think that you really agree with what I say." But "really" means "at heart" or "if you consider it again," since Clough proceeds to answer Price's conservative arguments from a liberal or "labor" point of view. In any event, this item is closely related to No 29.

1847?   "An ill world . . ."   31

This 4-page Bodleian MS was written in a mood of extreme depression. The imagery of its attack on humanity is reminiscent of Swift. Miss Barish (see No 27) dates the item c June 1847, primarily because "the paper is in every respect identical with that" used for No 30: "These are the only two such similar pieces of paper I have found in the Clough MSS and they are alike in size, watermark, color, and maker's imprint as well as ink and handwriting."

1847 November 2   Letter in The Spectator xx (Nov 6 1847) 1066, signed Alpha 32

This and the next item are reprinted in *SPW* 273–275 under the incorrect title of "Two Letters about Francis W. Newman's *The Soul*": see our comment on No 33.

—— November 15   Letter in The Spectator xx (Nov 20 1847) 1118, signed Alpha   33

This and the previous letter belong to the correspondence in *The Spectator* from Oct 23 to Nov 20 1847, discussing F. W. Newman's lecture at London University on Oct 13 1847, "The Relations of Free Knowledge to Moral Sentiment." Newman's answer to Clough's letters is in *C* I 187–190. This and an unpublished letter from Bonamy Price to Clough, Dec 5 1847, in the Bodleian Library, make the identification of Alpha almost certain.

1849–51?   A Sunday Morning Contemplation   34

Five meditations in a Bodleian MS of 18 pages. The main theme is the weary disillusion with reading and speculation that appears in *Amours de Voyage*, Canto III, letter X (1849) and "Say, will it, when our hairs are gray?" (1851). The reference to the intersection of Goodge Street and Bemers Street may suggest the period when he was Principal of University Hall, Oct 1849 – Jan 1852.

1850–51?   Letter on Christian Socialism, signed Citoyan   **35**

Reprinted in *SPW* 243–248.

This Bodleian MS of 25 pages, some of which is missing, begins, "Gentlemen" [that is, the Council of the Society for Promoting Working Men's Associations, founded in 1850], and continues: "I am a fixed customer of two of your cooperative establishments, that of the working tailors at no   Castle St. Oxford St., & that of the Working shoemakers no   Holborn." Since the former was started at no 34 Castle Street on Feb 11 1850, and a splinter group on Oxford Street in October or November of that year, and the latter was set up in April 1850 at No 151 High Hoborn, the date we suggest seems reasonable. The reference to "your new periodical the Christian Socialist" shows that the Address was written after Nov 2 1850, when that journal first appeared.[17]

The Address is a criticism of Christian Socialism and the Cooperative Workshop movement, but from a moral rather than a political position: the end of evil and the regeneration of man will *not* be achieved by producer cooperatives. Politically, Clough was sympathetic, as his signature implies, though with characteristic flexibility he here mentions certain advantages in the system of competition which he usually attacked for the same reasons the Christian Socialists did (cf *C* ɪ 126–127, for example).

On May 31 1848 Clough had sent his remembrances from Paris (*C* ɪ 213) "to all my concitoyens at Oriel," and later referred (ɪ 216) to the letter Arnold wrote him addressed to "Citizen Clough, Oriel Lyceum, Oxford." (Cf Part I, No 26.)

1850–51?   "Review of Mr. Newman's *The Soul*"   **36**

No trace of this has been found in the obvious periodicals for 1849, when the book came out, or for 1850–1851. It was reprinted, or perhaps printed for the first time, in *PPR* ɪ 293–305 and again in *SPW* 277–286, but with the omission of six paragraphs that apparently do not belong to the review: see No 55 below.

A MS of almost exactly the same text as that in *PPR*, which is in Clough's hand, is in the Bodleian Library. A first draft in the form of musings and jottings is in the *1850 (Venice) Notebook* (Bodleian MSS, English Poetry, d. 133) among what appear to be monologues for *Dipsychus*. This is not surprising since the review is closely connected with the poem, and in particular with the "Epilogue."

1850–51?   A letter contributed to *Oxford University Commission. Report of Her Majesty's Commissioners Appointed to Inquire into the State, Discipline, Studies, and Revenues of the University and Colleges of Oxford* (London, 1852), in the section called *"Evidence"* (separately paged) ɪɪ 211–216   **37**

Reprinted in *SPW* 303–316.

The date is based on the fact that Clough refers (p 211) to the commissioners' questions of Nov 18 1850, and that the commission (see minutes, p ix) finished reading all replies by Feb 25 1851. There are comments on his letter by R. H. Hutton in *C* ɪɪ 321 and in an anonymous review in the *North British Review* xvɪɪɪ (1853) 11–14, written by Clough's friend John Conington: see *The Wellesley Index to Victorian Periodicals, 1824–1900*, ed W. E. Houghton (Toronto and London 1966) ɪ 676. Clough's personal copy of the *Report* is now in the Widener Library at Harvard (Educ 4000.5A), but without marginalia: cf *C* ɪɪ 467.

Five of the following items (Nos 38–41 and 48), and probably Nos 42–44, were originally lectures given by Clough at University College, London, in 1851 or 1852 when he was Professor of English Language and Literature. In a letter which Mrs Clough wrote to Charles Eliot Norton, Nov 2 1864 (Harvard MSS), she spoke of her desire to publish "some lectures or notes for lectures on Poets" which her husband had given as "Professor of English Literature at University Col-

---

[17] See Charles E. Raven, *Christian Socialism, 1848–1854* (London 1920) 150–151, 158, 182–184, 197–198, 200–202, 378. Miss Barish (see under No 27) considers Clough's letter a reply to the leading article in the first issue of *The Christian Socialist*.

lege"; [18] and on William Allingham's advice, she wished first to print some of them in a magazine like the *Atlantic Monthly*. She mentioned those on "Coleridge Southey and Wordsworth," on Dryden, and on Swift; and in a later letter, Jan 26 1865, added the "Development of Literature" (No 48). By that date she had sent Nos 38–41 and 48 to Norton for him to revise as he pleased and submit to whatever journal he thought best. On Dec 20 1864 she wrote of them: "They are not worked up & rounded off into essays but bear the marks of jottings down & almost spoken interruptions & have the repetitiousness of lectures. I have tried as much as I can to cut out these things, but am afraid of meddling too much."

At the opening of the lecture on Scott (No 43) Clough remarked: "With the names of Cowper & Burns I might perhaps fitly close a series of lectures which took their commencement with Dryden. From Dryden to Cowper are words which may stand not unfairly to represent one great age, the 2nd age of English Literature. . . . The canons of writing and laws of Taste which were established by Dryden were still unrepealed & still in force when the Task came forth from Olney." He decides, however, to look briefly into "the age which we ourselves are living in."

1850–51? Dryden and His Times   38

Six lectures in a MS of 114 folios in the hand of Blanche Clough at Harvard. The reference in Lecture I (fol 6) to Wordsworth's decease "a few months ago" (he died on April 23 1850) suggests autumn 1850 or early in 1851 as the date.

Part of Lecture I (fols 14–20) was printed in *PPR* I 329–333 and *PR* 325–329, with the title "On the Formation of Classical English: An Extract from a Lecture on Dryden." Lectures I and VI are reprinted in *SPW* 85–106.

1851–52? Jonathan Swift   39

Three lectures, the first incomplete, in the Bodleian MSS entitled by Mrs Clough: "Fragment of Lecture I on Swift" (22 pages), "Lecture II on Swift" (58 pages), and "Lecture III on Swift" (41 pages). At the start of a lecture that followed Lecture III (No 38 below) Clough speaks of having tried to characterize Swift in the last *four* lectures, so that either the fourth is missing, or the first was really the second, a possibility supported by Clough's reference at the very beginning to the " 'Journal to Stella,' from which I have given you extracts." Mrs Clough, writing to Norton on Jan 26 1865 (Harvard MSS), says that the lectures on Swift were "originally 4."

Another MS in the hand of Blanche Clough is at Harvard in 42 fols. It is a revised version in which the division marks and outline notes have been deleted, and lecture phrasing altered or omitted, in preparation for publication in America as a single essay. It appeared in the American edition of *Good Words* VII (Jan 1866) 40–48, and was signed "By the late A. H. Clough." It was not in the English edition.[19]

—— —— Lecture on Period following on Swift   40

This also exists, like the lectures on Swift, in manuscripts at the Bodleian (32 pages) and at Harvard. In the Harvard MS Mrs Clough has written at the top of fol 1: "(This may be left out if preferred)," which we take to be a note to Norton.

—— —— Wordsworth as Man & Poet   41

An initial draft of this essay, running to 32 pages in Clough's hand, entitled by Mrs Clough "Lecture on Wordsworth, unpublished," is at the Bodleian. After the opening 6 pages

[18] Clough was elected to the professorship Dec 7 1850 and resigned in Sept or early Oct 1852: see *Henry Crabb Robinson on Books and Their Writers*, ed Edith J. Morley (3 vols, London 1938) II 706, 720.

[19] We wish to thank Professor Trawick for calling this to our attention.

on Wordsworth, it attempts to place him in his time by describing the work of Coleridge and Southey, with briefer reference to that of Scott, Rogers, Campbell, and Moore. It ends with the word "Preliminary."

The revised and final draft, also in Clough's hand and at the Bodleian, uses the first six pages of the first draft; it contains 52 fols and is reprinted in *SPW* 107–122.

Another and shorter version, of 27 fols in the hand of Mrs Clough, designed for publication in a periodical (see note preceding No 38), was sent by her to Norton and is now at Harvard. The purpose of the abridgement was simply to remove a few paragraphs that contained amplifications or illustrations which were unnecessary in an essay to be read; and in our opinion nothing significant was omitted. The arrangement of the material near the end is an improvement. In her letter of Dec 20 1864 Mrs Clough tells Norton that last week she posted "a copy of the lecture on Wordsworth." The Harvard MS bears the postmark, "New-York Dec. 29 Br. Pkt.," which is the date of its arrival in New York by British packet. Minor revisions in the hand of Norton are mainly designed to remove the phrasing of a lecture, in further preparation of the MS for publication as a review. At the end of the text, Norton has written (fol 28 verso): "Running Title-Wordsworth. Art. — The Works of William Wordsworth. In six volumes. 16 mo. Boston: Little, Brown and Company." The reference is to the edition of Wordsworth in "The English Poets" series edited by F. J. Child, first published in 1854 and reissued in 1864 (in seven volumes, not six).

The revised MS then appeared in the *North American Review* (of which Norton was now editor), c (April 1865) 508–521. Since the article was unsigned, the false impression was given that it was written by a living critic who supposedly had the Wordsworth edition before him. The published text was slightly shorter than Mrs Clough's MS. Norton deleted a few sentences, but far more serious, he crossed out several paragraphs at the very end (the last five in *SPW* 122), thus closing the essay on a much more critical note than Clough intended. Unfortunately, the *North American* text was used by Mrs Clough when she reprinted the essay, without reference to any previous publication, in *PPR* 309–325 and *PR* 305–321, where it is called "Lecture on the Poetry of Wordsworth." There is a critical comment on this essay by Henry Sidgwick: see Part III, No 123, either p 383–384 or 84–85.

1851–52? William Cowper   *42*

The lecture on Cowper in the Bodleian MSS was published with only minor revisions (blanks left for proper names filled in, the paragraphing increased, a few words changed, and the short notes on Burns at the end omitted) in *Good Words* VII (Mar 1866) 208–212, signed, "By the late A. H. Clough."

In the plan made in 1859 by Clough and Thomas Arnold for continuing Johnson's *Lives of the Poets*, Clough was to do the Cowper: cf *C* II 566, 567.

—— —— Lecture on Scott   *43*

This lecture of 16 pages in the Bodleian MSS is probably the first of at least two lectures on Scott, since the survey of his life and work breaks off rather abruptly in 1805.

—— —— Lecture on Language   *44*

This Bodleian MS of one or perhaps two lectures begins with a characteristic salute to "human equality" (cf Nos 50 and 51) which leads into a passage on the importance of Teutonic languages and culture, especially German and English. Most of the MS discusses the history and "the genius of our tongue."

—— —— Poetry and Philosophy   *45*

This Bodleian MS of 2 pages, for which we have supplied the title, is reprinted in *SPW* 123. The tentative date is based on the possibility that the MS was connected with the London lectures.

—— —— Archytas of Tarentum   *46*

Fragment of 1½ pages in the Bodleian MSS on the theme that one must not act when angry. The similarity in paper and ink to the previous item, and the same use of classical instances to teach a moral truth suggest the same date.

—— —— Diogenes   **47**

A similar fragment of a page, using another classical anecdote to question whether salvation depends on the rites of any religious communion.

1852 The Development of English Literature   **48**

A lecture in MS of 70 folios in an unidentified hand and without title: Harvard MSS. Except for the last six folios, it was printed, with a few minor omissions, in *PPR* I 337–355 and *PR* 333–351, where it was called "Lecture on the Development of English Literature from Chaucer to Wordsworth," and dated 1852 (from the reference on *PPR* I 340 or *PR* 336). When Mrs Clough decided not to print the last six folios dealing with the nineteenth century, she made the title indicate the new terminal point. They are included in the text as reprinted in *SPW* 124–142.

These last folios (*SPW* 140–142) are an alternate ending in a separate blue book designed to take the place of the final paragraph in *PPR* I 355 or *PR* 351 where Clough refuses to carry the sketch any further. They were omitted by Mrs Clough, probably because they repeat materials in the Wordsworth lecture (No 41) on *PPR* I 314–315, 320–322 or *PR* 310–311, 316–318.

The lecture was first given at University College, probably on Thursday, Oct 14 1852, when Stanley Jevons wrote in his journal of hearing "the introductory lecture of the arts, by Professor Clough, on the Literature of England." [20] It was again delivered, apparently, and with some revisions, at Harvard on Jan 5 1853 (*C* II 361): see *PPR* I 188 or *PR* 195, where Mrs Clough rewrites Clough's statement of Dec 16 1852 from Cambridge that he is "to read that lecture here" (*C* II 349), to make him say he is "to read a lecture here on English literature." (The "that" of Clough's phrasing implies that the lecture was not a new one, and dovetails with my suggestion above about its first appearance.)

Later on, in 1854, when Norton was preparing an edition of Clough's poems, Clough sent him "the old Cambridge Lecture" to fill out what he feared would be too small a volume (*C* II 481). This may be the MS at Harvard, but since the alternate endings are both included, leaving the MS in need of an editor's hand, the Harvard MS is probably the one sent by Mrs Clough to Norton on Jan 26 1865: see our note preceding No 38.

The next four items (Nos 49–52), in the handwriting of Clough, carry the general title of "Letters of Parepidemus" in the Bodleian MSS. In a shorter form and reduced to three (Nos 50 and 51 have been combined), they were prepared for publication by Mrs Clough and sent to Charles Eliot Norton in 1865. This MS in her hand, is at Harvard, where it has been catalogued misleadingly as "Letters to various persons, from America and England." On January 26 1865, Mrs Clough wrote to Norton (Harvard MSS), "I have enclosed at last 3 imaginary letters written 1 on the voyage to America & 2 on arriving, which, if you don't think it possible to do anything with — you might perhaps like to see." She means, ". . . if you don't think it possible to publish them in a periodical:" see our note preceding No 35.

1852 November "Letters of Parepidemus on Board the Canada 1852"   **49**

This familiar essay in the form of a letter, reprinted in *SPW* 317–324, is partly made up of materials in *C* II 326–331. It is signed "Teelothen," which is a transliteration of τηλοθεν,

---

[20] *Letters and Journal*, ed his wife (London 1886) p 22. Jevons gives "the 15th, Thursday," but in 1852 Thursday was the 14th, and that date is confirmed in *Henry Crabb Robinson on Books and Their Writers*, II, 720, diary for "Oct 14th," 1852: "Then I came to the University College, where Clough, who had already resigned his professorship of English Literature, yet delivered his lecture prepared on the History of English Literature. But, admirable as the substance was, so ill delivered was this lecture that it gave little pleasure."

meaning "From Afar." This pseudonym was then replaced, apparently, by "Parepidemus" ("The Sojourner").

—— *November or December*   Letter of Parepidemus   **50**

This MS of only 4 pages and without signature seems to be incomplete and is probably a first draft of the next item, since the latter begins with another version of what he carried away with him from America twenty-five years ago. Here, in a discussion of the meaning of equality, he says he brought to England "a good deal of ineradicable republican sentiment."

—— ——   Letter of Parepidemus   **51**

This MS of 16 pages, signed "Parepidemus," is a continuation or a revision of the previous item. It was reprinted in *SPW* 249–255 under the title, "Might versus Right in Economics and Politics."

In this discussion of equality Clough strikes hard at political and economic injustice, and at the Carlylean doctrine of might makes right. In a sentence that links his left-wing politics with his distaste for luxury consumption, he says that what he carried away from the United States twenty-five years ago was "a sense . . . of natural equity between man and man, and a reluctance to take more than my fair share, so strong as to be apt at times even (This is perhaps a European possession) to pass into an Indisposition to claim of my own voice any share at all."

—— ——   Letter of Parepidemus from America. 1852   **52**

This MS of 6 pages is reprinted in *SPW* 256–257 under the apt title, "British and American Imperialism." Like No 50 it is unsigned and is probably incomplete.

1852? Observations of a Young Cur   **53**

A fable of 3 pages (Bodleian MSS) in the form of a dialogue between a young cur and his uncle, the "elderly sheep dog," on the subject of whether all dogs are equal "originally & in themselves." The discussion involves the relative effects of heredity and environment. The very tentative date is based on the fact that Nos 50 and 51 also deal with equality.

1852–53? Notes on the Religious Tradition   **54**

Reprinted in *SPW* 289–293. In a note to her reprints — *PPR* I 421–426 and *PR* 415–421 — Mrs Clough assigned the MS "to the last period of his life." But the MS is in the so-called 1852–3 (A) *Notebook* in the Bodleian: see *Poems* 474, 480. Both Trawick, *SPW* 339, and Mrs Clough in her note indicate that Clough associated these "Notes" with his poem, "What we, when face to face we see," *Poems* 61.

There is a comment on the "Notes" by J. A. Symonds in the *Fortnightly Review* IV n.s. (Dec 1868) 594–596, reprinted in his *Last and First* (New York 1919) 77–84.

—— Paper on Religion   **55**

This 4-page Bodleian MS was printed by Mrs Clough as part of No 36: *PPR* I 301 at the break, to 302 at the fifth line from the bottom; but it contains no reference to Newman's book and does not fit into the context. It may be complete as it stands, and is printed in *SPW* 287–288, as a separate item. Its skeptical view of the dogmatists and its reference to wider religious traditions seem to relate it to the previous item.

—— The Genius of Christianity   **56**

This short statement (Bodleian MSS), drawing an analogy between personal conversion and the conversion of the world through various events in the life of Christ, is placed here because it seems to illustrate the same theme that appears in No 54: that the religious tradition is not to be narrowly identified with the Christian tradition.

1853 Fragment of a lecture on the Iliad   **57**

This short MS (Bodleian) is very probably the lecture Clough started to write, with original translations, in Jan 1853 at Cambridge: See *C* II 361, 362, 365. His reference to "that civilisation which we commonly call European & which we might I suppose also call American," supports that hypothesis.

—— *April* "Oxford University Commission" being a review of *Report of Her Majesty's Commissioners Appointed to Inquire into the State, Discipline, Studies, and Revenues of the University and Colleges of Oxford* (London 1852) *North American Review* LXXVI (April 1853) 369–396   **58**

Because of its autobiographical nature, a small section of this review, p 390–393, was printed in *SPW* 324–327, as "A Passage upon Oxford Studies," and by Mrs Clough in *PPR* I 405–408 and *PR* 399–402, as "A Passage upon Oxford Studies: Extracted from a Review of the Oxford University Commissioner's Report, 1852." Cf *C* II 366, 369, 381, 383 (two references), 388, 389, 391, 411.

—— *July* "Recent English Poetry" *North American Review* LXXVII (July 1853) 1–30, being a review of Alexander Smith, *Poems* (1853); Matthew Arnold, *The Strayed Reveller and Other Poems* (1849) and *Empedocles on Etna, and Other Poems* (1852); William Sidney Walker, *Poetical Remains*, ed J. Moultrie (1852); and William Allingham, *Poems* (1850)   **59**

This review was largely, but not entirely, reprinted in *PPR* I 359–383 and *PR* 355–378. The discussion on p 27–30 of Walker and Allingham was omitted without mention and the essay called "Review of Some Poems by Alexander Smith and Matthew Arnold," so that few if any readers were aware that the essay was incomplete. Under Mrs Clough's influence, her title and text were unfortunately adopted for the only other reprint, in *Victorian Poetry and Poetics*, ed Walter E. Houghton and G. Robert Strange (Boston 1959) 381–389, but the text was there annotated. The complete text is in *SPW* 143–171. Clough refers to the essay in *C* II 417, 419, 424–434; and Arnold in *The Letters to Clough* 135, 140, 144.

—— —— "Recent Social Theories" *North American Review* LXXVII (July 1853) 106–117, being a review of Charles Eliot Norton, *Considerations on Some Recent Social Theories* (Boston 1853)   **60**

Mrs Clough printed "Extracts from a Review of a Work Entitled 'Considerations on Some Recent Social Theories'" in *PPR* I 411–417 and *PR* 405–412. The extracts omit all the quotations from the book, which were extensive, but include most of Clough's own text. The complete text is in *SPW* 258–269. For the attribution of the article to Clough and of the book to Charles Eliot Norton, see *C* II 434n and 435. There is a comment on the review by Arnold in *Letters to Clough*, p 138. Cf No 65.

—— —— "Letters of Parepidemus. I" *Putnam's Monthly Magazine* II (July 1853) 72–74   **61**

Reprinted in *PPR* I 387–395 and *PR* 381–389 and *SPW* 172–179 (where it is entitled "The Evolution of Criteria in Art and Literature"). Cf *C* II 398.

—— *August* "Letters of Parepidemus. II" *Putnam's Magazine* II (August 1853) 138–140   **62**

Reprinted in *PPR* I 395–402, *PR* 389–396, *Poems* 582–586, and in *SPW* 180–186 (where it is entitled "On Translating Homer"). Since this essay deals with the subject of Homeric translation, it may stem from the lecture Clough started to write in January of the same year: see No 57 and the references there to *Correspondence*. Clough found some misprints in the *Putnam* text: cf *C* II 463.

1853?   Review of a book on Progress   **63**

This incomplete MS (Bodleian), employing the editorial "we" of a reviewer and beginning, "Our friend in the little book before us," starts with a paragraph on progress, but its real subject is the dangers of sentimental benevolence, very much on the line taken by Carlyle in "Model Prisons," *Latter-Day Pamphlets*, 1850. The remarks on that topic in *PPR* I 166 and *PR* 171 give the gist of Clough's argument, and are in fact found almost verbatim near the start of the MS. Mrs Clough prints them as though taken from an undated letter to an unnamed correspondent. A passage on duelling has obvious relevance for *Dipsychus*, Scene VI.

The reference to a railroad from Boston to St. Louis and a telegraph line from Halifax to New Orleans suggests that the MS was written during Clough's stay in America, and probably in 1853. The same view of benevolence appears in his review of Norton's book (No 60) in July 1853: see *PPR* I 417 or *PR* 411–412.

1853 after July? Fragment on America   **64**

This Bodleian MS of 3 pages comparing America with Europe finds America weaker in knowledge but stronger in the power to act. The conjectural date is based on the fact that part of this idea appears in a letter to Norton written shortly after Clough's return to England: cf *C* II 460.

—— *October* A review of *Considerations on Some Recent Social Theories*, in *Westminster Review* LX (Oct 1853) 604–605   **65**

Clough was asked by John Chapman, editor of the *Review*, to contribute this notice of Charles Eliot Norton's book (cf No 60) to the article "Contemporary Literature of America": see *C* II 468.

1853–54? Letter on University Reform   **66**

A formal letter of 11 pages in the Bodleian MSS addressed "Sir" and apparently replying to what "Sir" has said, probably in a public letter to a newspaper or magazine. Reprinted in *SPW* 328–331. The subject is the need to improve "University teaching and University teachers" by changing regulations which at present are responsible for the low level of both. The occasion is the Oxford University Bill, introduced into Parliament by Gladstone in March 1854, and signed into law in August of the same year.

This letter may be regarded as a sequel to No 37; indeed, Clough mentions the 1852 *Report*, though not his own previous letter.

—— Petition on University Reform   **67**

This Bodleian MS of 4 pages is a rough draft, incomplete, of a petition which claims that "the University of Oxford is a National Institution . . . a place of general learning and education, not an ecclesiastical seminary," and that its educational duties are now being "inertly & unskilfully performed without respect to the extension of Modern Knowledge & Study." [21]

1858? Plutarch's Life   **68**

A Bodleian MS of 7 long sheets containing biographical material which was used almost verbatim for the Preface to No 72.

—— The Value of Popular History   **69**

A Bodleian MS of 13 pages that was later rephrased for the Preface to No 72. Clough argues that ancient historians still have their value as historians despite the fact that Niebuhr, Arnold, Mommsen, Thirlwall, and Grote have written more scholarly histories by using modern methods of research.

This item and the previous one have been placed together in the Bodleian MSS and given by Mrs Clough a single, ambiguous title: "Fragments of History from Plutarch." The titles adopted here were chosen by the present editors.

1859 June "Poems and Ballads of Goethe," *Fraser's Magazine* LIX (June 1859) 710–717, being a review of *Poems and Ballads of Goethe*, translated by W. E. Aytoun, D. C. L., and Theodore Martin (Edinburgh and London 1859). Signed A. H.C.   **70**

This essay on translation, reprinted in *SPW* 187–202, is related to Nos 62 and 71. The positive attribution to Clough is in *C* II 568.

[21] Miss Barish (cited in No 27) would date this petition c 1848 because "it appears to have been written while Clough was still at the university and before the Royal Commission had been established.

1859? On Poetical Translation   **71**

This Bodleian MS of 4 long sheets describing the difficulties of translation was probably the first draft of the opening paragraphs of No 70. A sizable section was printed, in a revised form, in that article, p 713 note; and at one point Clough refers to "the translator of whom we are about to speak," and proceeds to quote four lines that appear on p 713.

1859 Plutarch's Lives. The Translation called Dryden's. Corrected from the Greek and Revised by A. H. Clough (5 vols, Boston 1859)   **72**

Clough's "Preface, containing a Life of Plutarch," is on p v–xxix. There have been many reprintings of this work, which is still the standard translation. Comments by Clough, mainly on reviews, are in *C* II 570–576 and *PPR* I 229 *PR* 238; and by Arnold in *Letters to Clough* 151.

Specimen Pages of Plutarch's Lives, with the rest of the title as above, was issued at Boston in 1855. These 36 pages, containing most of the life of Pyrrhus, were a trial run-off, we assume, not intended for publication.

1860 Greek History from Themistocles to Alexander in a Series of Lives from Plutarch. Revised and Arranged by A. H. Clough (London 1860)   **73**

This selection of eight lives, which is arranged in chronological order to form, Clough says in his Preface, "a sketch of Greek history," and designed primarily as a school text, has also run through many editions. See Clough, *C* II 575–577, and Arnold, *Letters to Clough* 151–152. The Preface, p v–ix, is partly intended to counteract the fact that Plutarch, as Clough said elsewhere (*C* II 571), "is quite put out of fashion by Thirlwall, Grote, and Co." Its theme is described in No 69. He speaks in the Preface of wishing to prepare a second volume containing eight more lives.

*   *   *

Collected Editions

1869 The Poems and Prose Remains of Arthur Hugh Clough, ed by his wife (2 vols, London 1869)   **74**

In Volume I are reprints of Nos 29, 36, 41, 48, 54, 59 (incomplete), 61, and 62; and extracts from Nos 38, 58, and 60. See table of contents in No 87.

1888 Prose Remains of Arthur Hugh Clough, ed by his wife (London 1888)   **75**

Except for the omission of No 36, the prose in the previous item is here reprinted.

1964 Selected Prose Works of Arthur Hugh Clough, ed Buckner B. Trawick (University, Alabama 1964)   **76**

This volume, with introduction, notes, and bibliography, reprints everything in Nos 74 and 75, prints 14 items for the first time (all complete except No 38), and reprints 8 items not reprinted since this original publication by Clough, for the most part in out of the way places now hard to lay one's hands on. Moreover, it alone supplies the full and correct text for Nos 22, 36, 41, 48, 59, and 65.

Compared with this large contribution to the study of Clough, the erroneous titles for Nos 31 and 32 and some fumbles in the notes (pointed out by Kenneth Allott, *N&Q* 210, Aug 1965, 316–317), though certainly unfortunate, are of relatively minor consequence; they do not justify a review which highlights the faults, ignores the virtues, and concludes with a rude disparagement of the book in comparison with Mulhauser's editions of Clough.

The selection prints, under the heading of "On Language and Literature," Nos 3, 6, 11, 14i, 14x, 15i, 15vii, 20, 38 (lectures I and VI), 41, 45 (under another title), 48, 59, 61–62, and 70; under "On Economics and Politics," Nos 15iii, 22–27, 29, 30, 35, 51–52, 65; under "On Religion and Ethics," Nos 31–32, 36, 54, 55; under "On Miscellaneous Topics, Nos 7, 37, 49, 58 (but only a short section of it), 66.

APPENDIX

THIS appendix is a list of essays or speeches which Clough either wrote or may have written, but which have not been located in print or in manuscript. Items numbered 80–83, 85–91, are records of speeches he gave at an Oxford debating society called The Decade.

1835 July and October   Two prefaces to *The Rugby Magazine*   77–78
See the note before Part II, No 1.

1841 Autumn   On the Character of Saul   79
A paper written during the competition for the Balliol Fellowship. Reported by J. C. Shairp in R. T. Davidson and William Benham, *Life of Archibald Campbell Tait* (2 vols, London and New York 1891) I 72. Tait thought the paper "the best and most original thing he had ever known in any examination."

Between 1843 and 1848   Speech on "the future politics of the world, the connexion of the world and of the Church"   *80*
Reported by Frederick Temple to Mrs Clough on Feb 8 1862: see Arnold's *Letters to Clough* p 21, n 5. Temple said: "The grandeur of the thought and the splendour of the language quite carried [me] away." This may be the same as No 88.

Between 1843 and 1845   Speech on the motion: "That Tennyson was a greater poet than Wordsworth"   *81*
Reported by J. C. Shairp in *PPR* I 25 and *PR* 26, where the date is suggested; and in the *Christian Remembrancer* XLIV (Jan 1863) 65–66; reprinted in the *Living Age* LXXVI (Feb 21 1863) 393–394, where the motion is worded, "That Alfred Tennyson is the greatest English poet of the age."
According to the latter writer (who may be R. W. Church: see Part III, No 93), Clough undertook to oppose the resolution only when Matthew Arnold, who was to have championed Wordsworth, was unable to attend.

———   Speech on the motion: "That the character of a gentleman was in the present day made too much of"   *82*
Reported in some detail by Shairp, *PPR* I 25–26 and *PR* 26–27.

1844 or 1845   Speech in favour of Lord Ashley's Ten Hours Bill, attacking the principle of Laissez-faire   *83*
See Thomas Arnold, "Arthur Hugh Clough: A Sketch," *Nineteenth Century* XLIII (Jan 1898) 107. Clough's anti-laissez-faire point of view is in *C* I 128, 130, 148.

1844–48   Lectures at Oriel, probably on classical subjects   *84*
Cf *C* I 135, 138, 169.

1846 February 14   Speech on the motion: "That means ought to be adopted by the Legislature for recognising formally the social and political importance of the manufacturing interest"   *85*
Reported by John Conington, *PPR* I 31 and *PR* 32, and in the *Christian Remembrancer*, cited in No 81, 66–67, reprinted in the *Living Age*, p 394.

1846 June 9   Speech on the motion: "That any system of moral science, distinct from a consideration of Christianity, is essentially imperfect"   **86**

Reported by Conington, cited in No 85, who added that Clough eventually moved a rider: "But the existence of moral science is recognized and presupposed by the idea of a revelation."

1847 March 6   Speech on the motion: "That the study of philosophy is more important for the formation of opinion than that of history"   **87**

Reported by Conington, *PPR* i 32 and *PR*, p 33.

—— *May*   Speech on the subject: "The advisability of a separation of Church and State"   **88**

See Mrs Rosslyn Wemyss, *Memoirs and Letters of Sir Robert Morier* (2 vols, London 1911) i 37. This may be the same as No 80.

1848   Speech on "the social questions so prominent at the time of the Revolution of 1848"   **89**

Reported by George David Boyle, *Recollections* (London 1895) 124, where he says: "It was a marvellous speech, and his words as to the duties of property sank into my soul. I have never forgotten them. He concluded with an allusion to a fine passage in *Sartor Resartus*, where the aristocracy are spoken of as preserving their game."

1848?   Speech on "property and its distribution"   **90**

In a letter to Mrs Clough, April 16 1866, now at the Bodleian, G. D. Boyle wrote: "Of a speech made in the Common Room of Exeter at a meeting of the Decade, on the great question of property and its distribution, I can say with perfect truth, that one hearer at least felt that evening that a new view of life and his fellow human beings had been presented to him and that a lesson of earnest sympathy with the working man of England had not been read in vain." This speech may be the same as No 89; if not, its similar subject suggests a similar date.

1847 and 1848   One or two other speeches at The Decade   **91**

Conington, *PPR* i 31–32 and *PR* 33, reported that there were "five" speeches "in 1847 and the early part of 1848." Three have been accounted for (Nos 87, 88, 89) and perhaps a fourth (No 90).

1851–52   A lecture on Swift at University College   **92**

See No 39 above.

—— ——   A lecture on Scott at University College   **93**

See No 43 above.

—— ——   A lecture on Coleridge at University College   **94**

See note preceding No 38.

—— ——   A lecture on Southey at University College   **95**

See note preceding No 38.

There are remarks in the *Correspondence* or in Mrs Clough's "Memoir" (Part III, No 112) which suggest that between 1848, when Clough resigned his Oriel Fellowship, and August 1853, when he undertook the heavy task at the Education Office, he may have written some essays that have escaped notice. On Sept 4 1848 he said (*C* i 217) he might not write any more verse, but had "a notion for Essays." On Jan 8 1852, after he had lost the Professorship at Sydney, Bonamy Price urged him to write for the *North British Review* (*C* i 302–303), sending him a list of likely subjects and promising to write to A. C. Fraser, the editor, in his behalf.[22] In her "Memoir" (*PPR* 1 43 and *PR* 45) Mrs Clough says that Clough wrote "several articles" while in the United States for the *North American Review, Putnam's Monthly Magazine,* "and other magazines." But only articles listed in the two periodicals that are named are known to exist, viz: Nos 41, 58–62. On November 1st (1854) Harriet Martineau wrote to John Chapman, editor of the *Westminster Review,* that if he lost some old contributors like J. A. Froude, W. R. Greg, and F. W. Newman, "Surely Congreve, Clough, Payn, and others will more than compensate." [23]

[22] A search in the National Library of Scotland and in the Fraser Papers (privately owned) for correspondence between either Clough or Price and A. C. Fraser proved fruitless.

[23] Bodleian MS Eng. Lett. d. 2, fols 177–178. No 65 in 1853 is Clough's only known contribution to this quarterly.

Part III: Biography and Criticism

IN BRINGING TOGETHER the following biographical and critical materials on Clough, we have used all previous bibliographies that have carried entries pertaining to Clough: the Ehrsam, Deily, and Smith, *Bibliographies of Twelve Victorian Authors* (No 328 below); the supplement by Fucilla (No 337); the two collected *Bibliographies of Studies in Victorian Literature*, one covering 1932–44, the other 1945–54 (Nos 352 and 405); the third and fifth volumes of the *Cambridge Bibliography of English Literature* (Nos 341 and 414); the chapter by A. McKinley Terhune in *The Victorian Poets: A Guide to Research* (No 407); and the annual bibliographies for the Victorian Period since 1956 in *Modern Philology, Victorian Studies,* and *Publications of the Modern Language Association.* Besides these sources we have added from our own research many new articles, essays, and reviews.

A special feature of the present bibliography is the inclusion of many references to Clough in Victorian biographies, memoirs, diaries, and collections of letters, some of them unpublished, together with quotations from the most important. In addition, we have identified the authors of a large number of anonymous articles and reviews, and given the evidence for their authorship. In this connection, we have corrected a number of attributions that have been wrongly made in the past.

Two other matters may require a further word. First, our choice of a chronological rather than an alphabetical order rests on the belief that the former is more helpful to those wishing to trace the historical evolution of critical opinion and scholarly investigation and the extent of activity in these studies in any given period. Consequently, whenever the same essay has appeared in more than one place, the earlier (or earliest) source is given first. In addition, when it has proved feasible in the case of letters, memoirs, journals, diaries, etc, dates of specific entries concerning particular events in Clough's life or the dates of important letters have been used rather than the publication date. Second, the annotations of selected items are meant to supplement the purpose cited for our choice of the chronological method; the comments will, we trust, indicate the particular direction of the essay, review, or study, its contribution to Clough scholarship, and its value in the light of present-day opinion.

Finally, we make no claim to have included *everything* ever printed about Clough. We have not searched extensively through British and American newspapers; we have omitted many reviews of books like Lowry's *Letters of Arnold to Clough* and Woodward's *The Doctor's Disciples* not bearing directly on Clough, some notices of books about Clough that seemed perfunctory, and a few references that were of no scholarly or critical value. Some of the items in Part III have already been listed in *Innocent Victorian* (No 500). Anyone who discerns a valuable item which we have missed in urged to send it to us so that it may appear in a supplement or later edition.

1829–61
Clough, Arthur Hugh. *Letters and Remains* (For Private Circulation Only) (London 1865)   1
Besides the correspondence and poetry, this volume, ed Mrs Clough, apparently in consultation with others, contains biographical information by Clough's wife and sister, recollections by his friends, and critical commentary on his poetry and thought. Especially noteworthy are the remarks on *Dipsychus* and the two "Easter Day" poems, 145–146.

—— *The Poems and Prose Remains, with a Selection from His Letters*, ed his wife (2 vols, London 1869)   2
In this edition the interspersed biographical material of the previous item has been expanded and brought together into a formal "Memoir," ɪ 1–54, and the number of letters has been increased. (For comment on the "Memoir" itself, see No 112, and for Symonds' assistance, Part I, No 87.)

1830, 1841
Tait, Archibald Campbell. *Life*, ed R. T. Davidson and William Benham (2 vols, London and New York 1891) ɪ 40, 72, 107   3
Of special interest is Shairp's account of Tait's "furious" reaction to Clough's second class degree in 1841: "They had not only a first rate scholar, but a man of original genius before them, and were too stupid to discover it."

1836
Northcote, Sir Stafford. *First Earl of Iddesleigh*, ed Andrew Lang (2 vols, London 1890) ɪ 26–27   4

1836–42, 1856
Lake, William Charles. *Memorials*, ed Katharine Lake (London 1901) viii, 12, 22, 26, 29, 35, 37, 47n, 55, 72, 85n, 88, 192   5
Mainly about Clough's Balliol career; brief mention is made of his work as Secretary to the Military Education Commission: "Clough particularly is invaluable."

1837–40
Jowett, Benjamin. *The Life and Letters*, by Evelyn Abbott and Lewis Campbell (2 vols, London 1897) ɪ 50, 53, 88 (See also Nos 12, 413)   6

1837–62
Clough, Arthur Hugh. *The Correspondence of Arthur Hugh Clough*, ed Frederick L. Mulhauser (2 vols, Oxford 1957)   7

These volumes contain 279 complete letters and 292 partially printed letters; the 740 other letters in the Clough collection that have been omitted from this edition are listed in the "Catalogue of All Known Letters," Appendix III, II 622–649. Among the correspondents included in the published letters are Emerson, Carlyle, Tom and Matthew Arnold, W. G. Ward, J. A. Froude, C. E. Prichard, Edward Hawkins, C. E. Norton, Thackeray, Geraldine Jewsbury, Charles Kingsley, J. C. Shairp, J. P. Gell, J. N. Simpkinson, Thomas Burbidge, R. H. Hutton, Longfellow, F. J. Child, Florence Nightingale, William Allingham, and James Russell Lowell. Of special interest are the letters received by Mrs Clough after her husband's death from F. W. Newman, Emerson, and Jowett. (For comment on the editor's introduction see No 419.)

1838–45

Ward, William George. In Wilfred Ward, *William George Ward and the Oxford Movement* (London 1889) 67, 100, 104–112, 397, 405, 429   **8**

Their friendship and Clough's reaction against Ward are discussed by the latter, esp 104–112.

1839–43

Coleridge, John Duke. *Life and Correspondence*, written and ed by Ernest Hartley Coleridge (2 vols, London 1904) I 54, 77, 93, 101, 130, 134, 146   **9**

1840–61

Shairp, John Campbell. In William Knight, *Principal Shairp and His Friends* (London 1888) xiv, 33, 40, 49, 53, 54, 55, 63, 73, 87, 88, 106, 113, 205, 244   **10**

Excellent for conveying the deep impression that Clough was able to make on some of his contemporaries. "It was for [Clough] more than any of the others that Shairp then felt that idealising hero-worship, which generous young men, of imaginative susceptibility, feel for the genius of their contemporaries." In later years, in conversations that went back to his Oxford friends, "the name that most affected [Shairp] was Clough's."

1841

Stanley, Arthur Penrhyn. *Life and Correspondence*, ed Rowland E. Prothero and G. G. Bradley (2 vols, London 1894) I 306   **11**

Stanley complains of the uncongenial atmosphere at Oxford and indicates his regret over Clough's loss of the Fellowship at Balliol.

1844, 1862

Jowett, Benjamin. *Letters*, arranged and ed by Evelyn Abbott and Lewis Campbell (London 1899) 159, 177 (See also Nos 6, 413)   **12**

The first reference is to Clough's approval of Jowett's candidacy for the Moral Philosophy Professorship; the second to Clough's death and Jowett's visit to the widow. "He was a real poet, and when his remains are published, will be acknowledged to have so been by the world."

1845–68

Arnold, Matthew. *The Letters of Matthew Arnold to Arthur Hugh Clough*, ed Howard F. Lowry (New York 1932)   **13**

Letters 1 to 57, covering the period from 1845 to 1861, are, with exception of letter 31, from Arnold to Clough. [Letter 31 is from Clough to Arnold.] The last five letters (58–62) are from Arnold to Mrs Clough, written after the death of Clough, between 1861 and 1868. (For comment on the introduction by Lowry, see No 311.)

1847

Northcote, Sir Stafford. Letter to Gladstone in John Morley, *The Life of William Ewart Gladstone* (3 vols, London 1903) I 329   **14**

Northcote described Clough as "a very favourable specimen of a class, growing in numbers and importance among the younger Oxford men, a friend of Carlyle's, Frank Newman's, and others of that stamp; well read in German literature and an admirer of German intellect, but also a still deeper admirer of Dante; just now busily taking all his opinions to pieces and not beginning to put them together again; but so earnest and so good that he might be trusted to work them into something better than his friends inclined to fear."

1847–49

Morier, Sir Robert. *Memoirs and Letters*, ed Rosslyn Wemyss (2 vols, London 1911) I 37, 75, 76, 82   **15**

In a letter from Balliol, dated May 9 1847, Morier cites Clough as the "next best speaker" of the Decade, the best being Conington. The subject he heard being debated was the advisability of a separation of Church and State, and he was struck by the fact that all these "first-rate" men, however different in principle, all seemed to argue that this separation must take place sooner or later. Also mentioned in other letters are Clough's *Bothie* and his trip to Rome.

1847–72

Emerson, Ralph Waldo. In *Emerson-Clough Letters*, ed Howard F. Lowry and Ralph L. Rusk (Cleveland, The Rowfant Club 1934)   **16**

Letters 1–33 are between Emerson and Clough, covering the period from 1847 to 1861. Letter 34 (1862) is from Emerson to Mrs Clough; letter 35 (1862), Emerson to C. E. Norton; letter 36 (1866), Emerson to Mrs Clough; letter 37 (1872), Emerson to Mrs Clough. Emerson's delight in the *Bothie*, his disappointment over the ending of the *Amours*, and his grief at the news of the death of Clough are of special interest.

1848

[Brief Review of *The Bothie of Toper-na-Fuosich*] in "Publications Received," *Spectator* XXI (Dec 2 1848) 1166   **17**

The entire review is as follows: "A long story of some Oxford students, who went to the Highlands of Scotland to combine relaxation and study; but one of them falls in love with a Scotch lassie, whom he finally marries. As a tale, the piece has little interest; and the school-like incidents and persons by which it is sought to be varied are of an unattractive kind, intended to be natural, but only trivial. In prose, such a story, treated in such a way, would scarcely have been ventured upon; and it seems difficult to understand why plain prose should be thought the better for being turned into prosaic verse. At first view *The Bothie of Toper-na-Fuosich* looked like some Oxford satire; but if it does cover any occult meaning, it is confined to the initiated." For Clough's remark on the review, see *C* I 240.

Kingsley, Charles. *His Letters and Memories of His Life*, ed his wife (2 vols, London 1877) I 181, 191   **18**

The first reference is to two remarks about the *Bothie* in letters to J. M. Ludlow, one dated July 1848, the other undated but probably written about the same time; the second is to a letter to John Conington, December 19 1848, in which Kingsley refers to reviews that they both were doing for *Fraser's*: "So if you will keep your trumpet for 'Ambarvalia,' I will celebrate the birth of the 'Bothie' with penny whistle and banjo." (See Nos 29 and 32.)

1848–52

Froude, James Anthony. *A Biography, 1818–1856*, by W. H. Dunn (2 vols, Oxford 1961, 1963) I 95–96, 98–100, 130, 173, 224–225   **19**

For comments and letters on Clough's thoughts and activities during these years; for other references of lesser importance see Dunn's index. See also Herbert Paul, *The Life of Froude* (London 1905) 39–40, 41–44, 58, 59, 66, 129, 433.

Both books, on pages 224 and 40 respectively, contain the informative letter that Froude wrote to Clough about the *Bothie*: "I was for ever falling upon lines which gave me uneasy twitchings. . . . As to the story, I don't the least object to it on the *Spectator's* ground [cf No 17]. I think it would not have done in prose. Verse was wanted to give it dignity. But if we find it trivial, the fault is our own varnished selves. We have been polished up so bright that we forget the stuff we are made of."

Robinson, Henry Crabb. *On Books and Their Writers*, ed Edith J. Morley (3 vols, London 1938) II 682, 684, 686, 692, 693, 713–715   **20**

Especially significant for commentaries on Clough at University Hall. For other more general references see the index, III 1006.

1848–53
Emerson, Ralph Waldo. *Journals*, ed E. W. Emerson and W. E. Forbes (10 vols, New York 1909–14) VII 453, 560; VIII 16, 375–377, 388   **21**

The entries cover the years from Emerson's first meeting with Clough to his regret over Clough's departure from America.

Thackeray, W. M. *Letters and Private Papers*, ed Gordon N. Ray (4 vols, Cambridge, Mass 1945) II 456–457, 463–464, 578, 580–581; III 109n, 166n   **22**

Of special interest are Thackeray's praise of the *Bothie*; his suggestion that Clough was "crossed in love"; and his reference to Clough's "religious scruples." Thackeray wrote to Clough on November 24 1848: "I have been reading the Bothy [sic] all the morning and am charmed with it. . . . Your description of the Sky & the landscape — and that figure of the young fellow bathing shapely with shining limbs and the blue sky for a background — are delightful to me."

1848–56
Carlyle, Thomas. *Life*, by David Alec Wilson (6 vols, London 1923–1934) IV 53, 395; V 33, 174, 221   **23**

1848–62
Allingham, William. *Letters to William Allingham*, ed H. Allingham and E. B. Williams (London 1911) 44, 78, 152–165, 286   **24**

1849
Bagehot, Walter. In William Irvine, *Walter Bagehot* (London 1939) 21, 40–41, 64, 138, 164, 173, 200, 206; and in Alastair Buchan, *The Spare Chancellor: The Life of Walter Bagehot* (London 1959) 40, 48–56 passim, 75, 97, 114, 138, 142, 207   **25**

These studies stress the fascination that Clough had for Bagehot. Of special interest in both, pages 41 and 50–51 respectively, is the important letter of March 1 1849 in which Bagehot writes to R. H. Hutton: "Clough you would like very much, I think. He is a man of strong, and clear though not very quick intellect: so that I feel like a gnat buzzing about him. He has a great deal of imagination, and has written a good deal of poetry; a proportion of which is good, though he unfortunately has been in the Highlands and talks of barmaids and potato-girls and other operative females there in a very humiliating manner as it seems to me though Roscoe [William Caldwell] defends it. You would, I think, agree with me in thinking that his mind was defective in severity of moral feeling and in the conception of law generally as applied to morals. But he is evidently a man of great honesty and moral courage with an immense deal of feeling. C. Prichard says his mind was injured he thinks by an overstrained asceticism when he first knew him at Oxford, and has never recovered from the evil."

Bristed, Charles A. "Oxford Hexameters," *Literary World* (New York) IV (June 1849) 493–494, a review of the *Bothie*, signed C. A. B.; reprinted in his *Pieces of a Broken-Down Critic* (4 vols in one, Baden Baden 1858) I 215–220   **26**

Browning, E. B. *Letters*, ed F. G. Kenyon (2 vols, London 1897) I 426, 429 **27**

In two letters to Miss Mitford, Mrs Browning prefers the *Bothie*, with its "vigour and fresh-ness," to the poems in *Ambarvalia*. "[The *Bothie*] strikes both Robert and me as being worth twenty of the other little book, with its fragmentary, dislocated, unartistic character."

"Clough's Poems," *The Rambler* IV (July 1849) 201–205 **28**

[Conington, John?] [Review of *Ambarvalia*] in "Recent Poetry, and Recent Verse" *Fraser's Magazine* XXXIX (May 1849) 580–585 **29**

Kingsley's letter to Conington (cited in No 18) suggests that the latter wrote this article.

Emerson, Ralph Waldo. ["Review of 'The Bothie of Toper-na-Fuosich'"] *Massa-chusetts Quarterly Review* II (March 1849) 249–252; reprinted in *Uncollected Writings* (New York 1912) 23–25 **30**

In this very favorable comment on the *Bothie*, Emerson cites its "solid subject-matter, real and lifelike figures." He also recognizes the serio-comic nature of the piece, calling attention to the "singular charm" of the Homeric iteration, "half-comic, half-poetic."

"English Hexameters," *The Literary Gazette* LXVI (Aug 18 1849) 606–607 **31**

A highly unfavorable review of both the content and form of the *Bothie*. After quoting some lines from the banquet scene, the reviewer comments: "Of such materials is the whole com-posed, and often beautiful ideas made almost ludicrous by affectations, absurd terms, and ridiculous versifying."

[Kingsley, Charles] "*The Bothie of Toper-na-Fuosich*," *Fraser's Magazine* XXXIX (Jan 1849) 103–110; same in *Living Age* XXI (May 5 1849) 197–202 **32**

For the authorship see Kingsley's letter to Conington (cited in No 18); Clough's *C* I 240; and Margaret F. Thorp, *Charles Kingsley, 1819–1875* (Princeton 1937) 91, 92, 192.

Kingsley praises the poem for its subject-matter, form, and spirit; he is particularly impressed by the latter: "There runs through the poem a general honesty, a reverence for facts and nature — a belief that if things are here, they are here by God's will or the devil's, to be faced man-fully, and not to be blinked cowardly; in short, a true faith in God." His defence of the meter is unusual; most critics were annoyed by Clough's hexameters.

Martineau, James. *Life and Letters*, ed James Drummond and C. B. Upton (2 vols, London 1902) I 246 **33**

Clough's appointment as Principal of University Hall is noted.

Mitford, Mary Russell. *Correspondence with Charles Boner and John Ruskin*, ed Elizabeth Lee (Chicago n.d.) 139–140 **34**

In a letter to Boner, September 10 1849, Miss Mitford speaks of Clough's poems as being "painfully skeptical"; but nevertheless he is "a fine poet," "a poet in the highest sense."

[Notice of *Ambarvalia*] in "Poetry of the Million," *The Athenaeum* No 1111 (Feb 10 1849) 135–136 **35**

Powell, Thomas. "Thomas Burbidge and Arthur A. [sic] Clough," *The Living Authors of England* (New York 1849) 86–94 **36**

[Review of *Ambarvalia*] *The Guardian* IV (March 28 1849) 208–209 **37**

The writer prefers Clough's *Ambarvalia* to the *Bothie*. If less witty and amusing than the pastoral, it is "far more powerful, . . . more profound, more interesting, more rich in 'the thoughts that shake mankind.'" Perhaps most significant is the reviewer's recognition of Clough's par-ticularly effective techniques: his apt metaphors, precise diction, suitability of style to thought. Clough's greatest liability is the "morbid self-consciousness" displayed in the poems, from which "weariness and vexation can only ensue."

[Review of *Ambarvalia*] *The Literary Gazette* LXV (April 21 1849) 292–293 **38**

"*Arcades ambo,* and a queer couple," the review begins, and this sets the tone for the entire piece. The reviewer quotes "Away, haunt not thou me" as a specimen of Clough's "passable verse," but then gives *Natura Naturans* as an example of the "trash" Clough can write.

[Review of *Ambarvalia*] *Spectator* XXII (Jan 20 1849) 65 **39**

The reviewer sees more promise in *Ambarvalia* than in the great mass of verses that continually comes before him. The main characteristic of each poet is "a crude poetic power, which probably seems greater than it really is, from the vagueness both of subject and thought in which it is shrouded." This "careless obscurity" is more visible in the poems of Clough; Burbridge's are more complete as regards structure and form, but whether he has at bottom so much power as Clough is "a moot point." The greatest significance of this "brief notice" lies in the reviewer's recognition of what has been to many the chief attraction of Clough's poetry; a sincere, whole-hearted concern with truly significant subjects expressed in subtle, often irregular, verses. The question of Clough's "artistry" has been one of the recurring themes in the critical tradition.

Robinson, Henry Crabb. *Diary, Reminiscences, and Correspondence,* selected and ed by Thomas Sadler (2 vols, London 1869) II 383, 384–385, 389 **40**

Comments on the *Bothie* and on Clough's character.

Trevelyan, G. M. *Garibaldi's Defence of the Roman Republic* (2nd ed, London 1907) 93, 110n, 147, 150–151, 207 237 **41**

[Whewell, W. H.] "Dialogues on English Hexameters," *Fraser's Magazine* XXXIX (March 1849) 342–347 **42**

For the authorship see Isaac Todhunter, *William Whewell* (London 1876) I 292.

1849–52

Bagehot, Walter. *Life* by Mrs Russell Barrington (10 vols, London 1915) X 180–183, 278, 353–354, 361 **43**

The first item is an account of Clough's influence on Bagehot and their close friendship during the time that Clough was at University Hall.

1849–58

Brookfield, Jane Octavia. In Charles and Frances Brookfield, *Mrs. Brookfield and Her Circle* (2 vols, New York 1905) II 295, 389, 400, 458 **44**

1849–61

Espinasse, Francis. *Literary Recollections and Sketches* (London 1893) 362–365 **45**

A good description of Clough at the time of his visit to Manchester and Rochdale in 1849: "I remember him well with his fresh-coloured face, boyish-looking yet anxious, his rather stalwart Lancashire figure, encased in a loosely-buttoned black frock coat, and altogether with an aspect partly that of a cleric, partly of an athlete."

1849, 1861 or 1862

Carlyle, Thomas, and J. A. Froude. In Froude, *Carlyle's Life in London* (2 vols, London 1884) I 457–458; II 243–244; in Chapters XVI and XXV respectively **46**

The first reference (1849) contains both Froude's and Carlyle's favorable estimates of Clough, Carlyle regarding him as "a diamond sifted out of the general rubbish-heap." The second, in either 1861 or 1862, is Carlyle's reply to Froude's request for a few words to serve as a memorial to Clough; it reads in part: "A man more vivid, ingenious, veracious, mildly radiant, I have seldom met with, and in a character so honest, modest, kindly. I expected great things of him."

1849–62
Carlyle, Thomas. *Correspondence of Thomas Carlyle and Ralph Waldo Emerson, 1834–1872*, ed C. E. Norton (2 vols, London 1883) ɪɪ 174, 175, 180, 203, 219, 225, 229, 233, 245, 252, 281; superseded by *The Correspondence of Emerson and Carlyle*, ed Joseph Slater (New York and London 1964)   **47**

1850
[Notice of *Ambarvalia*] in "Recent Poetry," *Prospective Review* ᴠɪ (1850) 134–137   **48**

Rossetti, W. M. *"The Bothie of Toper-na-Fuosich," The Germ* ɪ (Jan 1850) 36–48 (See also No 487.)   **49**

1850–51
Hodgkin, Thomas. *Life and Letters*, by Louise Creighton (London 1917) 19–20   **50**
Hodgkin regarded the "lectures" in Clough's small class on Aristotle as "the most stimulating and fruit-bearing" of his whole college course.

Fry, Sir Edward. *A Memoir*, ed Agnes Fry (Oxford 1921) 42   **51**
Fry's account of his reading Aristotle under Clough: "Perhaps no class was ever more enjoyed by me or added more to my store of thought and to the cultivation of the habits of my mind."

1852
Jevons, W. Stanley. *Letters and Journal*, ed by his wife (London 1886) 22   **52**
A reference to Clough's lecture on "The Literature of England" (Part II, No 48): "I did not make much out of it."

1852–53
Wilson, James Grant. *Thackeray in the United States, 1852–53, 1855–56* (New York 1904) ɪ 12, 13, 15, 16, 155; ɪɪ 140–143   **53**

1853
Church, Dean [Richard William] *Life and Letters*, ed Mary C. Church (London 1894) 144   **54**
In a letter to Asa Gray, Church calls Clough "a noble-minded and most able fellow who has sacrificed a good deal — on very high principles, if not wisely."

Gray, Asa. *Letters* (2 vols, London 1893) 395–396   **55**

Howe, Julia Ward. *Reminiscences* (New York 1899) 184–187   **56**
A description of Clough's appearance and manner in America. "Mr. Clough was a delightful guest in all societies."

[Whewell, William] "English Hexameters," *North British Review* xɪx (May 1853) 143–146   **57**
For the authorship see Isaac Todhunter, *William Whewell* (London 1876) ɪ 294–295; and the *Wellesley Index to Victorian Periodicals*.

1853–54
Lowell, James Russell. *Letters*, ed C. E. Norton (2 vols, London 1894) ɪ 224, 234   **58**

1853–60

Milnes, Richard Monckton. *Life, Letters, and Friendships,* by T. W. Reid (2 vols, London 1890) I 463, 489, 490   **59**

1853–61

Norton, Charles Eliot. *Letters,* with Biographical Comment by His Daughter Sara Norton and M. A. DeWolfe Howe (2 vols, New York 1913)   **60**

The letters from Norton to Clough, covering the period from 1853 to 1861, are found in vol I; for comments on the relationship between the two men see passim I and II, esp I 86–90.

1853–78

Lowell, James Russell. *New Letters of James Russell Lowell,* ed M. A. DeWolfe Howe (New York 1932) 11, 52, 53, 238   **61**

Lowell mentions some lines from *Dipsychus* in a letter of 1878 to a correspondent (238); otherwise, all other references are to the years 1853–54.

1859–62

Tennyson, Alfred, Lord. *A Memoir* by Hallam Tennyson (2 vols, London 1897) I 450, 473–475, 480   **62**

The entries deal with Clough's opinion of Tennyson's "Idylls," his brief stays with the Tennysons during the summer of 1861, and Tennyson's expression of grief at Clough's death. One of Hallam Tennyson's statements is worth special notice: "Clough," said my father, "had great poetic feeling: he read me then his 'In Mari Magno' and cried like a child over it." According to W. M. Rossetti, *Pre-Raphaelite Diaries and Letters* (London 1900) 239, Tennyson found the language of the *Bothie* to be "execrable English."

1860

Spencer, Herbert. *An Autobiography* (2 vols, New York 1904) II 70–71   **63**

Spencer remembers Clough as a "very reserved, undemonstrative man, who usually took little share in general conversation."

1860–69

Eliot, George. *Letters,* ed Gordon S. Haight (7 vols, New Haven 1954–55) III 330, 466–467; IV 17; V 6   **64**

This edition supersedes that of J. W. Cross, *George Eliot's Life as Related in Her Letters and Journals* (3 vols, London 1885)

In a letter to Mrs Richard Congreve on February 23 1862, George Eliot writes: "I was much pleased with the affectionate respect that was expressed in all the notices of Mr. Clough that I happened to see in the newspapers. . . . That little poem of his which was quoted in the 'Spectator' [No 67] about parted friendships [*Qua Cursum Ventus*] touched me deeply."

1861

Arnold, Matthew. *On Translating Homer* (London 1861) in the *Complete Prose Works,* ed R. H. Super, vol I, *On the Classical Tradition* (Ann Arbor, Michigan 1960) Section III 150–151, 156   **65**

"Clough's Poems," *The Saturday Review* XII (Nov 30 1861) 564–565   **66**

A review of *Ambarvalia* and the *Bothie.* The writer sees the poems in the *Ambarvalia* volume as indicative of the "keen sense of difficulties," the "nice regard for the minutiae of truth," and the "manly love of duty" so characteristic of Clough. The *Bothie* is a "most delightful" poem, written in "a lucky hour," exhibiting a power of graphic description and a hearty love of nature.

[Hutton, R. H., and Thomas Hughes?] "Arthur Hugh Clough. — In Memoriam," *Spectator* XXXIV (Nov 23 1861) 1285–1286; same in *Eclectic Review* II n.s. (Jan 1862) 27–33   **67**

Many paragraphs are reprinted in Hutton's review of the 1869 volumes. See also R. H. Tener, "Richard Holt Hutton," *TLS* April 24 1959, p 241 (No 439), in which he presents evidence for Hutton's authorship for at least part of the article. The article is attributed to Thomas Hughes by C. E. Norton in his "Memoir" (No 84) and by Waddington (No 154). Lady Chorley (No 459), p 25n, follows Waddington in attributing it to Hughes, and then qualifies this in a letter to *TLS* March 9 1962, p 161, by stating that Hutton probably supplied the critical sections and Hughes the biographical ones. See R. H. Tener's letter in *TLS* March 2 1962, p 137, which called attention to Lady Chorley's attribution and prompted her reply.

Mainly biographical, filled with praise for Clough's intellectual and spiritual honesty. "He never flinched from the worldly loss which his deepest convictions brought on him." Some of his pieces will hereafter "hold their place beside those of Tennyson and Browning."

Stillman, William James. *The Autobiography of a Journalist* (2 vols, Boston and New York 1901) I 297, 299, 302–303   **68**

Clough is described by an artist commissioned by Norton to paint a small full-length portrait: "Of fragile health and with the temperament of a poet, gentle as a woman can be, he often reminded me of Pegasus in harness."

1862 [1]

"Arthur Hugh Clough" [Review of *Poems*] in *Church and State Review* I (Oct 1 1862) 240–241   **69**

Arnold, Matthew. *On Translating Homer. Last Words* (London 1862) in *The Complete Prose Works*, ed R. H. Super, vol I, *On the Classical Tradition* (Ann Arbor, Michigan 1960) 215–216   **70**

Bagehot, Walter. "Mr. Clough's Poems," *National Review* XIII (Oct 1862) 310–326; reprinted in *Literary Studies* (London 1879) II 257–281; and in *The Collected Works of Walter Bagehot*, ed Norman St John-Stevas (Cambridge Mass 1965) II 241–260   **71**

Bagehot, who knew Clough personally, spends much of his review of the 1862 volumes discussing the balance between Clough's spiritual and intellectual attitudes, attitudes fostered by his earlier years at Rugby and Oxford: "He had . . . by nature an unusual difficulty in forming a creed as to the unseen world; he could not get the visible world out of his head." His analysis of the poetry is limited mainly to the *Amours de Voyage*, which he cites as "a very remarkable description of this curious state of mind," but he mentions qualities that are found in many of Clough's other poems: his accurate depiction of states of mind, his irony, his "strong realism." The latter characteristic, especially, Bagehot emphasizes. "He saw what it is considered cynical to see, — the absurdities of many persons, the pomposities of many creeds, the splendid zeal with which missionaries rush on to teach what they do not know, the wonderful earnestness with which most incomplete solutions of the universe are thrust upon us as complete and satisfying."

Campbell, John McLeod. *Memorials*, ed by his son the Rev Donald Campbell (2 vols, London 1877) II 27   **72**

In a letter to Thomas Erskine, October 1862, Campbell speaks of finding in Clough's poems "the instinctive impatience of the doctrine of assurance which we were so familiar with thirty years ago."

[Chorley, Henry Fothergill] [Review of *Poems*] *The Athenaeum* No 1813 (July 26 1862) 107–109   **73**

---

[1] The volume of *Poems* under review in this year and the next is the first edition: see Part I, No 83 and No 84.

Attributed to Chorley by Leslie A. Marchand, *The Athenaeum* (Chapel Hill, North Carolina 1941) 192, 271.

Chorley regards the "Memoir" (see below, No 85) as an unsatisfactory apology for Clough's failure and views Clough's writing as "poor stuff," characterized by affectation, insincerity, and "namby-pamby sentimentalities."

[Clough, Anne Jemima?] "MS Life of A. H. Clough" [1862–63?], owned by Miss Katherine Duff, now on loan to the Honnold Library, Pomona College, Claremont, California   **74**

This 59-page manuscript, covering the period from 1837 to 1861, is thought to be the reminiscence of Clough's sister, written shortly after her brother's death, at the time when Mrs Clough invited people to send her their recollections of her husband.

"Clough's Poems," *The Saturday Review* xiv (July 26 1862) 109–110   **75**

[Collins, W. L.] "Clough's *Poems*," *Blackwood's Edinburgh Magazine* xcii (Nov 1862) 586–598   **76**

The review is assigned to Collins in "Blackwood's Contributors Book," National Library of Scotland; see also the *Wellesley Index to Victorian Periodicals*.

Curtis, G. W. "Death of Clough," *Harper's Magazine* xxv (Oct 1862) 710–711 **77**

[Findlay, John R.] [Review of *Poems*] *The Scotsman* (Aug 29 1862) 3   **78**

The authorship is revealed in Dr John Brown's *Letters* (see No 91), 156–157, where the review is discussed.

The Guardian xvii (Jan 22 1862) 76; (Jan 29) 100; (Feb 5) 124   **79**

The first two writers object to Stanley's statement (in No 87 below) that Clough broke away from the University and the Church with "delight"; the third supports Stanley's use of the term, providing that the expression conveys the idea of an intense feeling of relief. For further comments on these letters see Katharine Chorley (No 459) 103–104.

[Hutton, R. H.] "Mr. Clough's Long-Vacation Pastoral," *Spectator* xxxv (Jan 25 1862) 104–105   **80**

The greater part of this review of the *Bothie* is reprinted in Hutton's review of the 1869 volumes; also on the authorship see Tener (No 439).

[———] "Mr. Clough's Poems," *Spectator* xxxv (July 12 1862) 775–776   **81**

The basis for the attribution is the author's reference to the earlier memorial article on Clough (No 67), the central portions of which are acknowledged to be Hutton's.

In this review of the 1862 volume Hutton dwells at length on Clough's "suspense of mind," most evident in his early poetry, a quality which he condemns as "antagonistic to poetry." However, he finds the *Mari Magno* poems more harmonious and serene, showing less evidence of Clough's divided intellect; and he praises as "perhaps most perfect of all" those poems which retain *traces* of the poet's intellectual hesitancy "half-lost in a firm and certain purpose." Significant, too, are his comments on Palgrave's style. "Simpler words, a more natural manner of saying what he had to say, would have been far better." Should be read in conjunction with Palgrave's "Memoir" (No 85).

[Lewes, G. H.] "Clough's Poems," *Cornhill Magazine* vi (Sept 1862) 398–400 **82**

Lewes is listed as the author in the *Wellesley Index to Victorian Periodicals*.

Lewes insists that to talk of what he *might* have been, to say that he *lived* his poem instead of writing it, is "mere rhetorical evasion." As a man, he was doubtless lovable and loved; as a writer, he can claim but a modest place. He cites as the "nearest approach" to poetry the lyric *Qua Cursum Ventus*.

Masson, David. "The Poems of Arthur Hugh Clough," *Macmillan's Magazine* VI
(Aug 1862) 318–331   **83**

Masson views the poems as "representative relics" of Clough's spirit, and he tries to find in them the "peculiar cast" of his philosophy, the nature of his real thoughts. He discerns two periods in Clough's life. The first, the "speculative" or subjective, covers the time from Clough's twenty-first to his twenty-ninth year, the year he left Oxford; it is characterized by such subjective and confessional poems as *The New Sinai, In a Lecture Room,* and *The Questioning Spirit.* The second period, covering the rest of his life, is more "objective" than the first, and is characterized by poems which are "records of general feelings and impressions, or even small exercises of imagination on selected topics, rather than personal confessions or meditations." The passing of Clough from the "subjective" to the "objective" in the style and aim of his poetry is the main theme of the review: "It was as if, considering the nature of the speculations which had so long been occupying him, and which it was now becoming desirable that he should have done with in that form, and should pack up into a faculty for working and producing, he saw that he could not complete the packing up, or even honestly pack up at all, unless he transferred himself from Oxford, where there *are* rules of contraband, to that more general world where everybody may go about with packages and no one has a right to stop or examine them." Masson's understanding of Clough's thought and nature is evident throughout the essay, particularly in his insistence on the positive nature of Clough's "scepticism" and his concern to emphasize the imaginative and healthy quality of much of his poetry.

Norton, Charles Eliot. "Arthur Hugh Clough," *Atlantic Monthly* IX (April 1862)
462–469; reprinted in slightly different form as "Memoir" to *The Poems of
Arthur Hugh Clough* (Boston 1862) i–xxxvi   **84**

Even more eulogistic in tone than Palgrave's memoir, Norton's essay describes Clough's writings as "among the most precious and original productions of the time" and Clough himself as one who "lived to conscience, not for show." It offers the *Bothie* as evidence of its author's belief that poetry should deal with life in no "constrained, formal, and distant relations," but should "give expression to the thoughts and feelings most natural to us, and afford the solution, if it may be found, of our present doubts and daily perplexities."

[Palgrave, Francis T.] "Arthur Hugh Clough," *Fraser's Magazine* LXV (April
1862) 527–536; reprinted with some changes by Mrs Clough as "Memoir" to
The Poems of Arthur Hugh Clough (London 1862) v–xxiv; to the second edition (London 1863), with some minor variations, and to *The Poetical Works of
Arthur Hugh Clough* (London 1906)   **85**

Elegiac in spirit and eulogistic in tone. Palgrave at times shows a tendency to praise too highly both the content of the writing and the character of the subject and to pass too lightly over certain aspects of both. Indicative of the latter is his statement that "one feels a doubt whether in verse he chose the right vehicle." However, for an insight into Clough's nature and for an understanding of the motivation behind many of his acts, the essay is invaluable. Palgrave paints a fully rounded portrait of Clough, bringing out qualities so often missed in later ones: "youthful blitheness and boyishness of heart," "physical resolve and energy," "the sunny glance or healthy homely laughter"; and he clearly recognizes what might be called the guiding principle of Clough's life: his early learning to distrust a theory not resting on honest acceptance of our human nature.

[Sellar, W. Y.] "Clough's Poems," *North British Review* XXXVII (Nov 1862) 323–
343   **86**

Attributed to Sellar by William G. Blaikie, letter to A. C. Fraser, September 25 1862, Fraser Papers (privately owned): "We are to have" a paper "by Prof. Sellar on Clough" in the next issue; and by Waddington (No 154), p 148. See also the *Wellesley Index to Victorian Periodicals.*

S[tanley,] A. P. "Arthur Hugh Clough," *Daily News* (London) Jan 8 1862, p 2   **87**

An extract of this was reprinted in *The Guardian* XVII (Jan 15 1862) 49, and inspired three letters either agreeing or disagreeing with Stanley's remarks (see No 79 above).

Symonds, John Addington. *A Biography,* by Horatio Brown (London 1903) 132, 197, 310, 478 **88**

Whewell, William. "English Hexameters: Mr. Dart's Translation of the *Illiad,*" *Macmillan's Magazine* v (April 1862) 487–488 **89**

Z. "Sonnet on Clough," *Spectator* xxxv (July 12 1862) 774 **90**

1862–63
Brown, Dr John. *Letters,* ed by his son and D. W. Forrest (London 1907) 156–157, 161–162 (Cf No 78) **91**

In a letter to J. R. Findlay on September 30 1862 Brown writes: "I place Clough very high as an intellectual and moral *poet.*" To Professor Sellar on July 7 1863 he writes: "I send Mrs Sellar Clough's Poems and Memoir. I don't know when a book and *man* more laid hold on me."

1863
"Arthur Hugh Clough," *The Boston Review* III (March 1863) 132–138 **92**

The reviewer, regarding Clough as a representative doubter, calls the poems "sad" because of a "want of Christian faith." He honors Clough's noble honesty, but he regrets the misuse of his religious nature and warns against the evil influence of his poetry. "Clough's poems are often disfigured, many of them made obscure by the spirit of restless mental questioning." He recommends the *Bothie* because it is "full of frolicsome and hearty playfulness."

[Church, Richard William?] "Clough's *Poems,*" *Christian Remembrancer* xlv (Jan 1863) 61–89; same in *Living Age* lxxvi (Feb 28 1863) 391–407 **93**
Attributed to Church by Waddington (No 154), p 102.

[Hutton, R. H.] "Mr. Clough's Poems. New Edition," *Spectator* xxxvi (Oct 10 1863) 2604–2606 **94**

Many paragraphs are reprinted in Hutton's review of the 1869 volumes; see also Tener (No 439) on the authorship.

1865
Clough, Arthur Hugh. *Letters and Remains* (London 1865) (For a description of this volume see above No 1) **95**

1866
[Allingham, William] "Arthur Hugh Clough," *Fraser's Magazine* lxxiv (Oct 1866) 525–535 **96**

A sympathetic survey of Clough's life and poetry, mostly biographical, based on the *Letters and Remains* (privately printed, 1865) and on Allingham's personal acquaintance with Clough. Clough is described as an "Englishman of our own day with its novelties and problems, intellectual, cultivated, thoroughly honest and singleminded, and possessing moreover a marked degree of originality, which, after all is the truly interesting thing." Allingham views the poetry as an effective and characteristic expression of Clough's thought and experience, the emphasis being on "the matter and meaning" rather than on "mere beauty and melody." "He was comparatively inattentive to the subtle effects of language and metre, caring much for conveying his thought strongly and clearly, and but little for giving delight by the way." While much of the commentary in this essay is conventional and undistinguished, Allingham's recognition of Clough's preference for "intellectual" rather than "musical" poetry is worthy of note.

Allingham, William. *A Diary,* ed H. Allingham and D. Radford (London 1907) 143 **97**

For other less significant references to Clough see 57, 68, 72, 107, 108–109, 109, 129, 350; for Mrs Clough 86, 87, 89, 98, 102, 107, 166.

The most important entry, dated Monday, October 1 1866, is Allingham's critical estimate of Clough's poetry, which is in accord with that given in his *Fraser* article (see immediately above); he finds it "often too truthful to be good as art." "In everything, indeed, he aims at exactness, sometimes with too obvious an effort."

Arnold, Matthew. "Thyrsis," *Every Saturday* (Boston) I (March 10 1866) 278–280; and *Macmillan's Magazine* XIII (April 1866) 449–454; reprinted in *New Poems* (London 1867) 73–85   **98**
Arnold's moving elegiaic tribute to Clough, not to be read as biographical truth.

[Lowell, James Russell] "Swinburne's Tragedies," *North American Review* CII (April 1866) 544–555 (esp 545); reprinted in *My Study Windows* (London 1871) 210–226 (esp 211)   **99**
Lowell characterizes Clough's work as "the truest expression in verse of the moral and intellectual tendencies, the doubt and struggle towards settled convictions, of the period in which he lived." In two earlier essays Lowell makes mention of Clough. In "Cambridge Thirty Years Ago" (1854) he refers to Clough's finding in its intellectual atmosphere "a repose which recalls that of grand old Oxford"; and in "At Sea" (1854) he tells of Clough's [and Thackeray's] being driven to five meals a day for mental occupation aboard ship. For three other references to Clough see: his "Introduction" to *The Biglow Papers* (Second Series, 1867); his later essay, No 117 below; and his poem "Agassiz," dated February 1874, section III, stanza 5.

[Smith, William H.] " 'Dipsychus' and the Letters of A. H. Clough," *Macmillan's Magazine* XV (Dec 1866) 89–102   **100**
This review is attributed to Smith by Mrs Clough in a letter of February 27 1867 to C. E. Norton (cited in *C* II 647). In addition, George S. Merriam in "Preface" to *The Story of William and Lucy Smith* (New York and Boston 1889) cites Smith as the author. Louis Bonnerot, in his *Matthew Arnold, "Empedocle sur L'Etna"* (Paris 1947) wrongly attributes the article to Benjamin Jowett. (See also *Wellesley Index to Victorian Periodicals*.)

[Symonds, J. A.] "Clough's Life and Poems," *Cornhill Magazine* XIV (Oct 1866) 410–421; same in *Living Age* XCI (Nov 3 1866) 259–266; same in *Every Saturday* II (Nov 3 1866) 515–520; same in *Eclectic Magazine* LXVII (Dec 1866) 735–743   **101**
Symonds is cited as the author in the *Wellesley Index to Victorian Periodicals*.
J. C. Maxwell informs us that a Balliol College Library offprint of this essay records comments by Mrs Clough, Froude, and Henry Sidgwick; Sidgwick e g finds Part I of *Dipsychus* subtler, narrower, but therefore "more intensely concentrated" than Goethe's *Faust*.

1867
Elze, Karl. *Der englische Hexameter, eine Abhandlung* (Dessau 1867) 24–25, 32, 33, 36–37   **102**

[Norton, C. E.] "Arthur Hugh Clough," *North American Review* CV (Oct 1867) 434–477   **103**
For authorship see the published index of contributors to *North American Review*.
This review of the privately printed 1865 volume of *Letters and Remains*, mainly biographical, is highly eulogistic. Norton sees the poems as "the reflection of his soul": Clough's "liberal temper, his questioning habit of mind, his absolute devotion to truth, and his sense of many sidedness, are all expressed in his poems."

Swinburne, Algernon C. "Mr. Arnold's New Poems," *Fortnightly Review* VIII (Oct 1867) 414–445 (esp 434); reprinted in *Essays and Studies* (London 1875) 123–183 (esp 164); reprinted in *Complete Works*, ed Edmund Gosse and Thomas J. Wise, Bonchurch edition (London 1926) XV 62–119 (esp 100)   **104**

1868

Curtis, G. W. [Letter concerning Arthur Hugh Clough] in "The Old and the New," *Putnam's Magazine* n.s. i (Jan 1868) 6–7   **105**

Macdonald, George. *England's Antiphon* (London 1868) 327–328   **106**

Symonds, John Addington. "Arthur Hugh Clough," *Fortnightly Review* x (Dec 1868) 589–617; reprinted in his *Last and First*, ed Albert Morell (New York 1919) 63–137   **107**

It is obvious that the author, who aided Mrs Clough with the 1869 edition of the *Poems and Prose Remains*, not only sympathizes with the views of the poet, but is one of the few contemporary writers who seem to have understood his aims and ideas. Although Symonds states that he will "examine" the works, he concentrates almost solely on the *Amours de Voyage*, *Dipsychus*, and *Mari Magno*; and he discusses the matter rather than the manner of the poetry, taking up Clough's treatment of religion, love, and action or work. His analysis of Clough's religious position, in particular, is incisive and penetrating. In his discussion of Clough's "artistic qualities," to which he devotes only a little space at the end, he cites his intensity of passion, profundity of thought, and simplicity of form.

1868–69

Symonds, John Addington. *Letters and Papers*, collected and ed by Horatio F. Brown (London and New York 1923) 17, 18, 19–20, 25–26, 30, 30–31, 35–36, 39, 114   **108**

In a letter of May 14 1868 Symonds writes that Mrs Clough has asked him to help her in editing Clough's "Remains." "My Clough studies are likely to come to something." In a letter to Henry Sidgwick on September 5 1869 he analyzes a difficulty in criticizing Clough: "Clough is the crux of criticism. I am glad you have felt the pinch of him — the absolute impossibility of saying even what you think about him. It explains why all the notices he has had are so unsatisfactory; it also justifies the less articulate in their misappreciation of him, for where we cannot formulate we are apt to think there is nothing worth formulating."

1869 [2]

"Arthur Hugh Clough," *Every Saturday* viii (Oct 16 1869) 507–508   **109**

In this laudatory review of the 1869 edition the reviewer comments favorably on Clough's ability to impress people personally, commends his interesting letters, and praises his literary criticism and poetry; although he does find *Dipsychus* a failure — principally, one gathers, because of its sceptical ideas, for his only demurrer is against those who would sympathize with Clough's unorthodox attitude towards Christianity. The poet's "exaggerated belief in the isolated independence of the human mind" may have value in certain fields of philosophical analysis, but does not deserve any respect.

"Arthur Hugh Clough," *Once A Week* xxi (Oct 16 1869) 237–240   **110**

"Arthur Hugh Clough," *The Saturday Review* xxviii (Sept 18 1869) 383–385   **111**

Clough, Blanche Smith. "Memoir of Arthur Hugh Clough" in *Poems and Prose Remains* (2 vols, London 1869) i 1–54; same in *Prose Remains* (London 1888) 1–56   **112**

The bringing together of the various excerpts and recollections of the 1865 volume (No 1) into the more unified "Memoir" of this edition gives the essay a much more personal tone.

---

[2] The *Poems and Prose* under review in this year and the next is the edition of 1869 (No 2) edited by Blanche Smith Clough.

The effect is that of a tender and sometimes moving memorial, containing a wealth of biographical information and supplying an interesting commentary on different facets of Clough's writings and ideas. As one might expect, the approach is mainly eulogistic; but, on the whole, the comments on Clough's life and mind are surprisingly free from excessive sentiment or critical bias. There is no doubt that the unfortunate tradition that sees Clough's life broken off too soon "for the work he might have done" was fostered, perhaps even instigated, by this essay; but the pictures of Clough during his early years in America, then at Oriel and London, and finally in the Education Office and travelling abroad are revealing, and the intimate glimpses into his personal relations during his whole life are especially rewarding. One noteworthy omission in the 1869 "Memoir" is that of the remarks made on *Dipsychus* and "Easter Day," parts I and II, in the 1865 volume, p 145–146. Whether Symonds, who helped to edit the volumes (cf No 108 and Part I, No 87), was responsible for this omission is not known, but the comment in the 1865 volume on the second part of "Easter Day" reveals particulary well Mrs Clough's strong belief in her husband's own faith: "It shows that whatever his mood, and whatever his intellectual perplexities, the faith in God and in good, and the sense of the divine character of Christ, survived." The "Memoir" still remains the starting point for any study of Clough.

[Collins, Mortimer?]   [Notice of *Poems and Prose*] *British Quarterly Review* L
    (Oct 1869) 575–576   *113*
    Attributed to Collins on the basis of the note he wrote to the editor, Henry Allon, on August 18 1869 (Dr Williams' Library, London), asking if he might do a short review of the book.

Dowden, John.   "Arthur Hugh Clough," *Contemporary Review* XII (Dec 1869)
    513–524; same in *Living Age,* CV (April 2 1870) 56–72   *114*
    In this review of the 1869 volumes, Dowden's remarks on Clough's religious position are illuminating. While not denying Clough's sceptical habit of mind (the balance of the believing and the critical), and not agreeing with Clough's final spiritual position, Dowden does insist that Clough was not a "wavering doubter," as many claim. On the contrary, he finds: "His was no life of dreamy inaction, toying, *dillettante*-like, with the luxury of doubt. Not by a single act only, but by labours of his whole brief life, he vindicates for himself the character of one who was not a hearer merely, but a doer of the word that God spake to his heart." (On Clough's religious position, also see Nos 412 and 446.)

Hollings, H. de B.   [Review of *Poems and Prose*] *Academy* I (Oct 9 1869) 3–4 *115*

[Hutton, R. H.]   "Arthur Hugh Clough," *Spectator* XLII (Sept 11 1869) 1073–
    1075; same in *Living Age* CIII (Oct 23 1869) 197–201; same in *Eclectic Magazine* LXXIII (Dec 1869) 719–723; reprinted in slightly different form in *Essays Theological and Literary* (London 1871) II 368–391, Chapter VII, and in *Literary Essays* (London 1892) 286–309, Chapter VI   *116*
    Hutton's review of the 1869 volumes is a satisfying, well-written one; his criticism of the longer poems is sensitive and intelligent, particularly that of *Amours de Voyage:* "a poem brimful of the breath of his Oxford culture, of Cardinal Newman's metaphysics, of classical tradition, of the political enthusiasm of the time, and of his own large, speculative humour, subtle hesitancy of brain, and rich pictorial sense." One regrets that Hutton says so little about the lyrics, but even here, while obviously indicating his lack of admiration for them, he demonstrates his awareness of the principal appeal they may have for others in their introspective questionings and indirect portrayal of emotion. One of the finest contemporary appraisals of Clough.

Lowell, James Russell.   "On a Certain Condescension in Foreigners," *Atlantic Monthly* XXIII (Jan 1869) 82–94 (esp 90–91); reprinted in *My Study Windows* (London 1871) 54–82 (esp 73)   *117*
    Lowell conjectures that one day, perhaps, Clough's poetry will be found "to have been the best utterance in verse of this generation."

[Mozley, J. R.] "Clough's *Poems and Prose Remains*," *Quarterly Review* CXXVI
(April 1869) 348–353   *118*
This review is assigned to Mozley in the *Wellesley Index to Victorian Periodicals*.

[Review of Clough's *Poems and Prose*] *The Athenaeum* No 2181 (Aug 14 1869)
205–206   *119*

[Review of *Poems and Prose*] *The Guardian* XXIV (Oct 6 1869) 1111–12   *120*

[Review of *Poems and Prose*] in "Table-Talk," *Putnam's Magazine* IV n.s. (Dec
1869) 752–754   *121*
The reviewer finds a wide difference between Tennyson and Clough, precisely because, one
infers, the latter was "out of tune with his times" in poetry as well as criticism. "Easter Day,
is cited as the one complete poem of Clough's which gives expression to the severe and high
ideal he was growing toward.

Sidgwick, Arthur, and E. M. Sidgwick. *Henry Sidgwick* (London 1906) esp 141,
142, 193–195, 214–217   *122*
Of most importance is Sidwick's analysis of *Amours de Voyage*, sent to Mrs Clough as an
enclosure on April 2 1869, part of which reads: "There are several threads of scepticism skilfully
interwoven in this story; and especially in the controversy which Claude's intellect carries on
with love, on which the main interest centres, there are at least two distinct elements, which
we may describe as (1) controversy with the mode of selection; (2) with the fact of selection.
The first of these is neatly argued, and the sceptical arguments are reasonable enough; but
the second, into which the first plays, reveals to us a much rarer and profounder mood. . . . This
mood is, in the strict sense of the term, *philosophic*. It consists in devotion to knowledge, abstract
knowledge, absolute truth, not as a means for living happily, but as offering in its apprehension
the highest kind of life. It aspires to a central point of view in which there is no distortion, a
state of contemplation, in which, by 'the lumen siccum of the mind,' everything is seen precisely
as it is."

Sidgwick, Henry. "The Poems and Prose Remains of Arthur Hugh Clough,"
Westminster Review XCII (Oct 1869) 363–387; reprinted in *Miscellaneous
Essays and Addresses* (London 1904) 59–90   *123*
In his review of the 1869 volumes, Sidgwick comes closer than any of the other Victorian
critics to analyzing the "modern" elements in Clough's poetry. He mentions as the reasons for
the slow growth of Clough's popularity in his day the subject-matter and the style. The former,
being sceptical and introspective, was in advance of his age; the latter, having little superficial
brilliancy, depending for its appeal in a very delicate and precise adaptation of form to matter,
was slow in making itself felt and known. Getting even more to the heart of the matter, Sidgwick
points out that the complexity of Clough's thought and the intensity of his feelings, though they
may have prevented his practical success in life, are the very sources of his "poetic originality
and importance." *Easter Day* is singled out: "The complex and balanced state of Clough's
moods shows itself in an irony unlike the irony of any other writer." Although Sidwick tends
to underrate Clough's *Mari Magno*, his judicious comments on his earlier poetry make this
essay an important work among the critical writings on Clough.

1870
[Hutton, R. H.] "The Modern Poetry of Doubt," *Spectator* XLIII (Feb 5 1870)
166–167; same in *New Eclectic Magazine* VI (April 1870) 490–494; reprinted in
his *Aspects of Religious and Scientific Thought*, selected from the *Spectator*, ed
Elizabeth M. Roscoe (London 1899) 380–381   *124*

1871
Sass, G. H. "Arthur Hugh Clough," *Southern Magazine* IX (July 1871) 72–88 *125*

1873
Shairp, J. C. "Balliol Scholars 1840–1843," *Macmillan's Magazine* xxvii (March
     1873) 376–382   **126**

1874
[Brown, James B.] "Scepticism and Modern Poetry," *Blackwood's Edinburgh
     Magazine* cxv (Feb 1874) 223–231; same in *Eclectic Magazine* n.s. xix (April
     1874) 488–495; reprinted in slightly different form in his *Ethics and Aesthetics
     of Modern Poetry* (London 1878) 1–26 (esp 1, 20–26) where he uses the pseu-
     donym J. B. Selkirk. (See *Wellesley Index to Victorian Periodicals.*)   **127**

Dowden, Edward. In *Fragments of Old Letters: E.D. to E.D.W., 1869–1892*
     (London and New York 1914) 94–95   **128**
     In this letter of May 15 1874 Dowden says that he is planning a lecture or two on Clough;
and that he thinks Browning, Wordsworth, and Clough were more beneficent influences on
young college men ten years ago than Swinburne, Morris, and Rossetti are now.

1874, 1883
Domett, Alfred. *Diary, 1872–1885*, ed E. A. Horsman (London 1953) 126, 275–
     276   **129**
     After remarking, in 1874, that Southey's hexameters in his *Vision of Judgment* were the
best ever written in English, Domett adds, "except perhaps some of Clough's in *The Bothie.*"
In November 1883 he reports a conversation with Browning on the same topic: "I instanced too,
Clough's *Bothie*, in which the bounding and buoyant fluctuation and fluency of many of the
verses . . . are such as to make them, if not classic hexameters, something at least as good in vivid
rhythmic dance and music of metre. Clough's he liked better [than Southey's], but looked upon
his poem 'as not seriously attempting hexameters, but rather as burlesquing them.' But here
he was wrong, for Clough certainly attempts them seriously in the serious parts of his poem.
But he gives himself unbounded license, often retaining only a remote resemblance to the
original hexameter."

1875
Perry, T. S. "Arthur Hugh Clough," *Atlantic Monthly* xxxvi (Oct 1875) 409–
     418   **130**

1876
Stedman, Edmund C. *Victorian Poets* (Boston 1876) 243–244   **131**

1877
"Clough, Arthur Hugh," *Encyclopaedia Britannica* (9th ed) vi (Edinburgh
     1877)   **132**

Dowden, Edward. "The Transcendental Movement and Literature," *Contempo-
     rary Review* xxx (July 1877) 297–318 (esp 309, 315–316); reprinted in *Studies
     in Literature* (London 1887) 44–84 (esp 68, 78–80)   **133**
     Dowden recognizes the influence of Carlyle on Clough; and he rightfully points to Clough's
"susceptibility to various cross and counter influences" as the source of the special virtue of his
poetry. His later statements on Clough in his "Victorian Literature" (No 162) are essentially
similar to those in this essay.

Hutton, Richard Holt. "Walter Bagehot," *Fortnightly Review* xxviii (Oct 1877)
     453–484 (esp 466–469); reprinted with slight alterations as "Memoir" to Walter

Bagehot, *Literary Studies* (2 vols, London 1879) I ix–lxvii (esp xxxiii–xxxviii); see also G. B. Smith, "Walter Bagehot," *Fraser's Magazine* xix n.s. (March 1879) 298–313 (esp 301–302). **134**

Jerram, C. S. *"The Bothie of Tober-na-Vuolich,"* N&Q Dec 1 1877 p 435 **135**
This and Nos 137, 138, 139, 143, 144 discuss the meanings of the original and revised titles of the poem (cf Part I, No 70).

Mayer, S. R. T. "Charles Kingsley and Arthur H. Clough," *St. James's Magazine* xxxi (March 1877) 265–276 **136**

Pickford, John. *"The Bothie of Tober-na-Vuolich,"* N&Q Aug 4 1877 p 88; Sept 8 1877 p 198–199 **137**

Rigaud, Gibbes. *"The Bothie of Tober-na-Vuolich,"* N&Q Nov 17 1877 p 394–395 **138**

"Toper-na-Fuosich," N&Q Nov 17 1877 p 395 **139**

1878
[Lyttelton, Arthur T.] "The Poetry of Doubt — Arnold and Clough," *Church Quarterly Review* vi (April 1878) 117–139; same in *Living Age* cxxxvii (May 18 1878) 410–421; reprinted in his *Modern Poets of Faith, Doubt, and Paganism* (London 1904) 73–105 **140**
Wrongly attributed by Terhune (No 407 p 108) to John Pickford.
While Arnold and Clough seem to resemble each other as poets of doubt, they differ in their attitudes towards nature, truth and duty, human relations, and love. In each area, insofar as their poetry expresses a "scheme of life," Arnold in his self-centeredness stands self-condemned, while Clough, in proportion as he feels himself able to cling to something external to him, is "hopeful, energetic, and religious." Noteworthy, too, is the author's insistence on "humorous irony" as the distinctive quality of much of Clough's poetry.

Moggridge, M. W. "Idyllic Poetry," *Macmillan's Magazine* xxxviii (June 1878) 103 **141**

Seeburg, L. *Ueber Arthur Hugh Clough* (Göttingen 1878) **142**
A cursory survey of Clough's life and work, of little critical or biographical value.

Stratton, Thomas. *"The Bothie of Tober-na-Vuolich,"* N&Q Feb 9 1878 p 114 **143**

"Tober-na-Fuosich," N&Q March 9 1878 p 199 **144**

1880
Ward, Thomas H. "Arthur Hugh Clough," *The English Poets* . . . (London and New York 1880, first ed; London and New York 1893) iv 589–592 **145**

1882
Gardiner, Samuel R. " 'Hobbes' in Clough's 'Bothie'," *Academy* xxii (Dec 30 1882) 471 **146**
Identifies Hobbes as G. Ward Hunt, a member of the reading-party on which the *Bothie* was founded and afterwards Chancellor of the Exchequer and First Lord of the Admiralty.

Hutton, Richard Holt. "The Unpopularity of Clough," *Spectator* LV (Nov 25 1882) 1507–1509; same in *Living Age* CLV (Dec 23 1882) 764–767; reprinted in *Brief Literary Criticism*, ed E. M. Roscoe (London 1906) 304–315   *147*

Raising the question of Clough's unpopularity, Hutton seeks the answer by contrasting the poetry of Clough and Arnold. He points out that Clough's poetry has neither the "fanciful art" nor the lucidity of Arnold's, two qualities which lead to immediate popularity. But he agrees with Lowell (No 117) that in future generations Clough will rank among the highest of his time, even above Arnold, for having found a voice for his self-questioning age, a voice of great range and richness and of deep pathos. Clough's popularity will be as great as Arnold's, for his poetry, with its realism, its "direct, home-thrusting" questioning, its buoyant humor, reaches in its high points a rapture and exultation which are beyond those of Arnold's, though its music is "less carefully modulated," and its "pictures less exquisitely framed." A terse, provocative essay.

Morshead, E. D. A. [Review of No 154] *Academy* XXII (Dec 23 1882) 444–445 *148*

1883

Hamilton, A. H. A. "Clough's *Bothie*," *Academy* XXIII (Jan 6 1883) 11   *149*

An attempt to identify the men on whom the characters were founded. (Cf Nos 146, 155, 206, and C II 621.)

Haweis, H. R. *American Humorists* (London and New York 1883) 74   *150*

Hutton, Richard Holt. "The Poetry of Arthur Hugh Clough," *Fortnightly Review* XXXIX (June 1883) 790–807; same in *Living Age* CLVIII (July 7 1883) 3–14   *151*

[Norton, C. E.?] "Clough," *Nation* (New York) XXXVI (March 22 1883) 259–260   *152*

This review is ascribed to Norton in Poole's *Index to Periodical Literature*.
The reviewer finds Waddington's book (No 154) lacking in "keenness of critical insight" and failing "alike in vigor and in delicacy of touch." As for Clough, he was ahead of his time in his poetry and ideas.

[Notice of No 154] in "New English Books," *Literary World* (Boston) XIV (Feb 10 1883) 47   *153*

Waddington, Samuel. *Arthur Hugh Clough: A Monograph* (London 1883; some copies appeared in 1882)   *154*

Waddington's study, the first full-length volume on Clough, is a disappointing work. It adds nothing substantially to the understanding of either his poetry or his life, and much of the interesting information in it is that contained in the extracts that Waddington uses from articles by authors who, as he writes in his preface, were personally acquainted with the poet. There is little critical discussion of Clough's poetic theories and techniques, and his comments on Clough's thought and actions are inclined to be overly laudatory. Perhaps the most interesting chapter is the first, in which Waddington discusses Clough's ancestry and the influence of his mother.

—— "Clough's *Bothie*," *Academy* XXIII (Jan 6 1883) 11   *155*

Identification of characters in the *Bothie* (see No 149).

1884

"Collections toward a Bibliography of Arthur Hugh Clough," *Literary World* (London) XV (June 28 1884) 213–214   *156*

G. S. M. "Arthur Hugh Clough," *Literary World* (London) XV (Aug 23 1884) 279   *157*

Rhys, Ernest. "Introduction" to *The Bothie, and Other Poems*. Canterbury Poets
(London 1884) vii–xxii; reprinted in 1896   **158**

1885
Shepard, William. "Arthur Hugh Clough," *Enchiridion of Criticism* (Philadel-
phia 1884) 243–246   **159**

1886
Hutton, Richard Holt. "Amiel and Clough," *Spectator* LIX (Jan 9 1886) 42–43;
reprinted in *Criticisms on Contemporary Thought and Thinkers* (2 vols, London 1894) I 204–213; and in *Brief Literary Criticisms* (London 1906) 316–
325   **160**

1887
Bynner, C. N. "Arthur Hugh Clough," *Harvard Monthly* IV (July 1887) 177–
184   **161**

Dowden, Edward. "Victorian Literature," *Fortnightly Review* XLVII (June 1887)
835–867; reprinted with some changes in *Transcripts and Studies* (London
1888) 152–236 (esp 205–208) (See also No 133)   **162**

Hayward, Edward F. "Clough and the Poetry of Reaction," *The Unitarian Review*
XXVIII (Aug 1887) 131–142   **163**

Robertson, John M. "Clough," *New Essays towards a Critical Method* (London
1897) 301–330   **164**
  In this edition Robertson says that the essay on Clough was written in 1887.
  In the preface Robertson indicates that he is claiming "a status and a kind of recognition
that have not latterly been given" to Clough. In the essay itself he attempts to show that Clough
was "a great and original artist in fiction." Clough's poems in hexameters, the *Bothie* and
Amours de Voyage, ought to be classified as fiction rather than poetry. The *Bothie*, particularly,
is "an artistic success without parallel in its kind." There is "no piece of fiction in the language,
within similar compass, which can compare with this for quantity and quality, in its combination
of truth, force, and variety of character-drawing, truth of environment, depth of suggestion,
and range of association and sympathy." In both of these poems, the author concludes, "the
versifier has surpassed the existing prose fiction on its own ground." (For a rejoinder to Robertson's claims, see No 199 below.)

Stephen, Sir Leslie. "Arthur Hugh Clough" in *DNB* IV 583–584   **165**

1888
Patmore, Coventry. "Arthur Hugh Clough," *St. James's Gazette* (Aug 10 1888) 7;
reprinted in *Principle in Art* (1st ed, London 1889; London 1912) 106–112 **166**

"The Poems and Prose Remains of Arthur Hugh Clough," *The Saturday Review*
LXVI (July 7 1888) 25–26   **167**

1889
Bijvanck, Willem G. C. Essay on Clough, in *Poëzie en leven in de 19de eeuw*
(Haarlem 1889) 195–218.   **168**

Higgs, William. "Arthur Hugh Clough," *New Englander* LI (Oct 1889) 241–
255   **169**

Mayhew, A. L. "The Etymology of 'Clough,'" *Academy* xxxvi (Aug 31 1889)
137–138   **170**

Molloy, J. "Clough," *Academy* xxxvi (Sept 21 1889) 188   **171**

Murray, J. A. H. "Clough," "Clow," *Academy* xxxvi (Nov 23 1889) 341   **172**

Shairp, John Campbell. *Portraits of Friends* (Boston 1889) 195–212   **173**

Taylor, Isaac. "Clough," *Academy* xxxvi (Sept 7 1889) 154   **174**

1891
Johnson, Lionel. [Review of Matthew Arnold's *Poetical Works*] *Academy* xxxix
(Jan 10 1891) 31–32; reprinted with some changes in *Post Luminium: Essays
and Critical Papers*, ed by Thomas Whittemore (London 1911; New York 1912)
293–298   **175**
Johnson contrasts Arnold's meditative poems, which reveal his true humanism, with Clough's,
which he characterizes as "mournful, homesick, desultory, . . . touched with decay, because
they are composed without care, in no wide spirit of contemplation."

Noble, James A. "Arthur Hugh Clough," in *The Poets and the Poetry of the Century*, ed A. H. Miles (London 1891) iv 597–604; same in *The Poets and the
Poetry of the Nineteenth Century*, ed A. H. Miles (London 1905) iv 645–652 **176**

Sharp, Amy. "Arthur Hugh Clough," in *Victorian Poets* (London 1891) 121–
137   **177**

Swinburne, Algernon C. "Social Verse," *The Forum* xii (Oct 1891) 169–185;
reprinted in *Studies in Prose and Poetry* (London 1894) 84–109 (esp 104–105);
reprinted in *Complete Works*, ed Edmund Gosse and Thomas J. Wise, Bonchurch edition (London 1926) xv 264–288 (esp 283)   **178**
For other references to Clough by Swinburne see the index to *Swinburne's Letters*, ed C. Y.
Lang (Yale Univ Press 1959–1962) 6 vols. No 178 contains Swinburne's notorious limerick
on Clough. (For reply see No 309.)

1892
Boase, Frederic. "Arthur Hugh Clough," *Modern English Biography* (3 vols,
Truro 1892) i 654–655   **179**

Oliphant, Margaret. "Arthur Hugh Clough," in *The Victorian Age of English
Literature* (2 vols, New York 1892) ii 436–437   **180**

Small, Alex. "The Swan-Songs of the Poets," *Gentleman's Magazine* cclxxiii (Dec
1892) 574–577; same in *Living Age* cxcvi (Jan 21 1893) 254–256   **181**

Swanwick, Anna. "Arthur Hugh Clough," in *Poets the Interpreters of Their Age*
(London 1892) 367–375   **182**

1893
Johnson, Rossiter. "Clough and Hare," *Book Buyer* x n.s. (June 1893) 215 **183**

"The Religious Poetry of A. Clough," *Wesleyan Methodist Magazine* CXVI (1893)
513–520 *184*

1894
[Brief notice of No 186] *Nation* (New York) LVIII (June 28 1894) 485 *185*

[Clough, Blanche M. S., wife of the poet] "Preface," to *Selections from the Poems
of Arthur Hugh Clough* (Golden Treasury Series, London 1894) v–vi *186*
Signed B.M.S.C. She may also have written the notes, one of which is important: *Dipsychus*
is described (p 139) as a dialogue between "Dipsychus, the double-souled hesitating thinker,
and the practical cynic, called the Spirit."

"Clough's Poems," *Literary World* (London) XLIX n.s. (June 22 1894) 573–574 *187*

Mabie, H. W. "A Poet of Aspiration," *Outlook* XL (June 2 1894) 960–963; reprinted in *My Study Fire*, second series (New York 1894) 101–114 *188*

[Notice of No 186] "Minor Notices," *Literary World* (Boston) XXV (July 14 1895)
221 *189*

Williams, Francis H. "Clough and Emerson," *Poet Lore* VI (June – July 1894)
348–356 *190*

1895
Boyle, George Davis. *Recollections* (London 1895) 95, 123–125 *191*
See Part II, Nos 29, 89, and 90 for some quotations.

Hunt, T. W. "Skepticism in Modern English Verse," *Homiletic Review* XXIX
(March 1895) 216–221 *192*

Murray, J. A. H. "Clough and His Poetry," *Homiletic Review* XXIX (April 1895)
291–298 *193*

Scudder, Vida. "Arthur Hugh Clough," in *The Life of the Spirit in the Modern
English Poets* (Boston 1895) 265–268 *194*

1896
"Five Books of Song," *Literary World* (London) LIV n.s. (Nov 27 1896) 449–450,
includes a notice of *The Bothie, and Other Poems* (London and New York
[1896]) (See No 158) *195*

Hudson, W. H. "Arthur Hugh Clough," *Studies in Interpretation* (New York and
London 1896) 77–149 *196*
A fine survey of Clough's thought.

Saintsbury, George. *A History of Nineteenth-Century Literature* (New York
1896) 309–310 *197*

Steede, M. "Arthur Hugh Clough," *Temple Bar* CVIII (May 1896) 35–48 *198*

1897
"Clough and His Defender," *Academy* LII (Oct 2 1897) 260–261 (A reply to No
164) *199*

Clough, Blanche Athena. *A Memoir of Anne Jemima Clough* (London and New York 1897) *passim*   **200**

Forster, E. "Arthur Hugh Clough," *Academy* LII (Oct 23 1897) 331 (A reply to No 164)   **201**

Guthrie, William N. "Arthur Hugh Clough," *Modern Poet Prophets* (Cincinnati 1897) 102–109   **202**

Norton, C. E. "Arthur Hugh Clough," in *Library of the World's Best Literature, Ancient and Modern*, ed C. D. Warner (31 vols, New York 1896–1899) VII (1897) 3821–3828; (46 vols, New York 1902) IX 3821–3828   **203**

Statham, F. R. "Arthur Hugh Clough," *National Review* XXIX (April 1897) 200–212; same in *Eclectic Magazine* CXXVIII (June 1897) 743–751; same in *Living Age* CCXIII (June 26 1897) 857–865   **204**

1898
Armstrong, Richard A. "Arthur Hugh Clough," in *Faith and Doubt in the Century's Poets* (London 1898) 43–66; a portion of the same reprinted as "Clough, Arnold, and Newman," *Living Age* CCXIX (Oct 1 1898) 67– 70   **205**

Arnold, Thomas. "Arthur Hugh Clough: A Sketch," *Nineteenth Century and After*, XLIII (Jan 1898) 105–116; same in *Eclectic Magazine* CXXX (March 1898) 358–364; same in *Living Age* CCXVI (Feb 5 1898) 382–389   **206**
    The most interesting portions of this reminiscence are those in which Arnold describes Clough as he was "in the brimming fulness of his powers": facing the rush of the other side and struggling for the ball as goal-keeper at Rugby; "talking very brilliantly" on walking tours and long vacations; debating in a "rich, penetrating, original" strain as a member of the Decade; skiffing up the Cherwell or breakfasting in his rooms on Sunday morning and discussing the events of the day with the other members of the "little interior company" at Oxford. Perhaps most striking is the account of his reprimand of Matthew Arnold in 1858. Arnold's sketch is a fitting complement to the "Memoir" in the 1869 edition (No 112).

Max Müller, Frederick. *Auld Lang Syne* (New York 1898) 127–128   **207**
    Max Müller seems to confirm the implications of the letter from Clough to his sister, Nov 18 [1846?], *C* I 174–175, about an engagement or half-engagement. But the correct date of the letter *may* be 1851, in which case Blanche Smith would be the young woman referred to.

Mortimer, John. "Concerning Arthur Hugh Clough," *Manchester Quarterly* XVII (1898) 374–393   **208**

White, Greenough. *Matthew Arnold and the Spirit of the Age* (New York 1898) 8–16   **209**

1899
Hale, E. E. *James Russell Lowell and His Friends* (Boston 1899) 135–137   **210**

Lloyd, Richard J. "Arthur Hugh Clough," *Proceedings of the Literary and Philosophical Society of Liverpool* LIII (1899) 1–34   **211**

Palgrave, Francis Turner. *His Journals and Memories of His Life*, by G. F. Palgrave (London 1899) 6, 31, 36, 38, 41, 71, 107, 143, 166   **212**

Shindler, Robert. "Tennyson, Arnold and Clough," *On Certain Aspects of Recent English Literature*, Six Lectures (*Neuphilologische Vortrage und Abhandlung*, II, ed Wilhelm Vietor, Leipzig, London, New York 1902) 17–37   **213**

These lectures were delivered at Marburg in the summer of 1899 and according to the author were meant to present "the fairly accepted views of the subject" rather than to "express any original opinions of one's own." Clough and Arnold are discussed on p 28ff, most of the space being devoted to Arnold. Shindler sees them as both having "pretty much the same views of life," the dominant note of each being what we may call "the nostalgia of unbelief, the pain of decaying and dying faith."

1900

Arnold, Thomas. *Passages in a Wandering Life* (London 1900) 56–64   **214**

Butler, A. G. *The Three Friends: Story of Rugby in the Forties* (London 1900) 100–107 (See also No 396)   **215**

Gates, Lewis E. "The Return to Conventional Life," *The Critic* (New York) xxxvi (Feb 1900) 174–177; reprinted in *Studies and Appreciations* (New York 1900) 32–38   **216**

Tuckwell, William. *Reminiscences of Oxford* (London 1900) 97–98   **217**

1901

Bridges, Robert. *Milton's Prosody* (Oxford 1901) 106–110; also in rev final ed (Oxford 1921) 106–109   **218**

In his essay on the accentual hexameter, Bridges finds a great deal to praise in Clough's poems: "My quotations are from Clough because I have found him an exception, and am charmed with the sympathetic esprit of his *Bothie* and *Amours*, in which he has handled aspects of life, the romance of which is very untractable to the Muse, and chosen for them a fairly satisfactory, though not a perfected form. If Clough did not quite know what he was doing in the versification . . . , yet he of all men most certainly knew very well what he was not doing."

Marble, Annie Russell. "Messages of the Nineteenth-Century Poets," *Dial* xxx (Feb 16 1901) 97–99   **219**

Mount, C. B. "There Were Giants in the Land," *N&Q* Aug 31 1901 p 186   **220**

Waugh, Arthur. "Victorian Voices of Doubt and Trust," *Current Literature* xxxi (Nov 1901) 553–559; reprinted as "The Poetry of Reflection and Doubt" in *Reticence in Literature* (London 1924) 53–60   **221**

1902

["Clough-Arnold Memorial"] *Academy* lxiii (July 12 1902) 51   **222**

1903

Omond, T. S. *English Metrists* (London 1903) 53, 93, 95, 97, 102, 104; slightly expanded in the "recast" volume (Oxford 1921) 40, 156–157, 169n, 177–179, 284–285, 306, 308   **223**

Most of his attention is on Clough's hexameters: "Clough stands forth as a true though not a great poet and an independent investigator and experimenter; but his experiments were too often forced, being out of accord with natural English prosody."

1904

"Clough and Tennyson," *Academy* lxvi (Feb 20 1904) 205   **224**

Collins, J. C. "Clough and Tennyson," *Academy* LXVI (Jan 30 1904) 133   **225**

Conway, Moncure Daniel. *Autobiography* (2 vols, New York 1904) I 156, 278–280; II 74–106   **226**

Lewis, W. A. "Clough and Tennyson," *Academy* LXVI (Jan 16 1904) 82; (Feb 20 1904) 205   **227**

Page, Curtis H. "Clough," in *British Poets of the Nineteenth Century* (New York 1904) 687   **228**

1906
Benn, A. W. *The History of English Rationalism in the Nineteenth Century* (2 vols, London 1906) II 46–52, 426   **229**
Benn emphasizes Clough's scepticism, and to the extent that Clough refused to accept any arbitrary judgments about religious and philosophical matters he is right; but he fails to appreciate properly what Matthew Arnold called Clough's "prophet side."

Herford, C. H. *English Tales in Verse* (London 1906) liv–lvi   **230**

Sandford, E. G., ed. *Memoirs of Archbishop Temple by Seven Friends* (2 vols, London and New York 1906) I 44, 52–53, 90–91, 153, 162n, 242, 297; II 416 (For Sandford's "Appreciation," see No 233)   **231**

Winchester, Caleb Thomas. "Arthur Hugh Clough," *Methodist Review* LXXXVIII (Sept 1906) 716–732; reprinted in *An Old Castle and Other Essays* (New York 1922) 362–380   **232**

1907
Sandford, E. G. *Frederick Temple, An Appreciation*, with a Biographical Introduction by William Temple (London 1907) xxv, xxxii, 16 (See No 231)   **233**

Smith, Arnold. "Clough," in *The Main Tendencies of Victorian Poetry* (London 1907) 105–115   **234**

1908
Brooke, Stopford A. "Arthur Hugh Clough," in *Four Victorian Poets* (New York 1908) 30–55; reprinted 1910, 1913, 1964   **235**
Brooke praises Clough's poetry for its clarity, its "ceaseless change of mood within one atmosphere," its excellent, light-flitting, kindly humour, its veracity, its intensely-felt matter. He also takes issue with Palgrave's statement that one feels a doubt whether in verse Clough chose the right vehicle. Yet, despite this praise, Brooke denies Clough the name of major poet: he had no poetic genius, only a gentle and charming talent, and his poetry remains "in the porch, not in the temple of the Muses."

Hertwig, Doris. *Der Einfluss von Chaucers "Canterbury Tales" auf die englische Literatur* (Marburg 1908) 57–59   **236**

1909
Kellner, Leon. *Die englische Literatur im Zeitalter der Königin Viktoria* (Leipzig 1909) 384–386; revised as *Die englische Literatur der neuesten Zeit* (Leipzig 1921) 230–231   **237**

1910

C[hambers], E. K. "Clough, Arthur Hugh," *Encyclopaedia Britannica* 11th ed v
(New York 1910)   238

Chapman, Edward Mortimer. "The Doubters and the Mystics," in *English Literature in Account with Religion* (Boston 1910) 426–432   239

Milford, H. S. "Preface," to *Poems of Arthur Hugh Clough* (London 1910) i–xiv
                                                                         240
Milford's introductory essay is concerned mainly with a discussion of Clough's use of the
hexameter, particularly in the *Bothie*, which he considers a "noble poem." He is eager to justfiy
Clough's management of the accentual hexameter because he believes that Clough's importance
in English poetry is dependent largely on the *Bothie*, on "his having shown there, clearly enough
if imperfectly, the potentialities of the accentual hexameter." (For an answer to Milford see
No 246.)

Saintsbury, George. *A History of English Prosody* (3 vols, New York 1910) III
408–410   241

Smith, Goldwin. *Reminiscences*, ed Arnold Haultain (New York 1910) 72–73 242

Walker, Hugh. *The Literature of the Victorian Era* (Cambridge 1910) 455–
465   243

1911

Dakyns, Henry Graham. "Tennyson, Clough, and the Classics," in *Tennyson and
His Friends*, ed Hallam Tennyson (London 1911) 188–205   244

Huth, Alfred O. *Über A. H. Clough's "The Bothie of Toper-na-Fuosich."* Inaugural Dissertation (Leipzig 1911)   245
Huth's study is a useful, if not stimulating or critical, examination of various aspects of the
poem. He gives some attention to the characters, ideas, natural descriptions, personal and literary
influences, and the form, often citing what others have said about each of these. An appendix
compares the first and the revised forms of the *Bothie*.

Omond, T. S. [Review of No 240] *MLR* VI (Oct 1911) 539–541   246
Omond thinks that the "true English hexameter" has yet to be written, but he finds valuable
hints in the *Bothie* and *Amours de Voyage*.

1912

Dixon, William M. *English Epic and Heroic Poetry* (London 1912) 278   247

Jones, Dora M. "English Writers and the Making of Italy," *London Quarterly
Review* CXVIII (July 1912) 92–93   248

Lutonsky, Paula. *Arthur Hugh Clough.* (*Wiener Beitrage zur Englischen Phil-
ologie*, Bd XXXIX) Wien 1912   249
A competent survey of his life and work; of special interest are the points she makes regard-
ing similarities of certain scenes in *Dipsychus* and *Faust*, and the influence of the Tübingen
School on Clough's religious thought as reflected in *Easter Day, Epi-Strauss-ium*, and *The
Shadow*.

1913

[Brief review of No 255] *The Athenaeum* No 4495 (Dec 20 1913) 724   250

Cook, Sir Edward. *The Life of Florence Nightingale* (2 vols, London 1913)
    passim   **251**

Guyot, Edouard. *Essai sur la formation philosophique du poète Arthur Hugh
    Clough: pragmatisme et intellectualisme* (Paris 1913)   **252**
    Guyot's demonstration of Clough's "pragmatism" is too dependent on his own particular
definitions of terms to be entirely satisfactory; but his examination of *Dipsychus* as the poem
best illustrating Clough's "impassioned" analysis and his refusal to accept any belief merely for
convention's sake is more cogently presented and thus has greater validity.

Rhys, Ernest. *Lyric Poetry* (London 1913) 355   **253**

Schelling, Felix E. *The English Lyric* (Boston 1913) 223   **254**

Whibley, Charles. "Introduction" to *Poems* (London 1913) ix–xxxvii; reprinted
    in 1920   **255**
    Whibley's principal thesis is that Clough was not a great poetic artist because he was more
concerned to state his difficulties and ideas accurately than artistically. "His thoughts clamoured
so loudly for utterance that he could not control them, and instead of a great poet, he became,
so to say, the mouthpiece of his own doubting age." The discussion of the longer poems is devoted
largely to Clough's use of the hexameter, which he regards as largely unsuccessful. (For a
rejoinder to Whibley's estimate of Clough, see the next item.)

1914
"Arthur Hugh Clough," *Contemporary Review* cv (Feb 1914) 285–288   **256**
    This reply to No 255 claims that Clough possessed "in wonderful measure" the very qualities
that give the touch of immortality to Dante, Chaucer, Shakespeare, and Milton: the sense of
reality, the critical mind, the human fellowship, the power to subordinate art to creation, the
flood of thought. The final assertion: "He is a great poet, whose work will still be alive when the
large mass of nineteenth-century poetry will be as dead as the paper it is printed on."

B. "Russell Lowell on A. H. Clough," *Spectator* cxii (Feb 14 1914) 263–264 **257**

Gill, W. K. "A. H. Clough," *Spectator* cxii (Feb 28 1914) 346   **258**

"Poetical Works of Arthur Hugh Clough" [Review of No 255] *Spectator* cxii
    (Feb 7 1914) 230–231   **259**

Reed, Edward Bliss. *English Lyrical Poetry* (New Haven 1914) 178, 476–481,
    485, 547   **260**

Scott, Dixon. "Clough's Poems" [Review of No 255] *The Bookman* (London) xlv
    (Feb 1914) 270–271   **261**

"Thyrsis," *TLS* June 4 1914 p 271–272   **262**

1915
Hearn, Lafcadio. "Pessimists," in *Interpretations of Literature* (2 vols, New York
    1915) i 338–340, 341, 342, 343   **263**

1916
Clark, J. S. "Arthur Hugh Clough," *A Study of English and American Writers*
    (New York 1916) 512–521   **264**

Jones, W. Lewis. "Matthew Arnold, Arthur Hugh Clough, James Thomson," in *Cambridge History of English Literature* (Cambridge 1916) xiii Chapter IV; bibliography of Clough in the same volume by G. A. B[rown]   **265**

1918
"Eminent Victorians," *Spectator* cxxi (July 6 1918) 10   **266**

Strachey, Lytton. *Eminent Victorians* (London 1918) 174–175, 187 (in the chapter on Florence Nightingale); 234–236 (in the chapter on Dr Arnold)   **267**
A destructive caricature. (For a reply see No 309.)

Ward, Mrs Humphry. *A Writer's Recollections* (2 vols, London 1918) i 15–18, 26, 53, 63–64, 113–119   **268**
Important for the years at Oxford.

1919
Byrde, Margaretta B. "Arthur Hugh Clough," *The Chronicle* (NY) xx (December 1919) 234–242; reprinted in *Modern Churchman* x (May 1920) 80–93   **269**

Grey, Rowland. "The Poet of the Woman Worker," *Englishwoman* (Jan 1919) 29–33   **270**

Hodgson, Geraldine E. *Criticism at a Venture* (London 1919) 53–57   **271**

Nitchie, Elizabeth. *Vergil and the English Poets* (New York 1919) 217   **272**

Osborne, James I. *Arthur Hugh Clough* (London 1919, Boston 1920)   **273**
A generally sympathetic study, but undistinguished in both its biographical and critical portions. As biography, it lacks solidity and thoroughness; as criticism it lacks depth. At best, it may be regarded as a useful general introduction to the study of Clough's life and work.

Shackford, Martha Hale. "The Clough Centennary: His *Dipsychus*," *Sewanee Review* xxvii (Oct 1919) 401–410; reprinted with some revisions in *Studies of Certain Nineteenth-Century Poets* (Natick, Mass 1946) 47–55   **274**
The first important study of *Dipsychus*. The author recognizes the source of Clough's poetic power in his "eternal protest against spiritual ease and smugness" and analyzes *Dipsychus* from this point of view, calling it a "critique of pure worldliness." Especially helpful to the modern reader are her remarks on the Byronic elements in the poem and her emphasis on the irony that underlies the entire work. "For those who enjoy paradox, antithesis, feigned cynicism, the play of concealed weapons, Clough offers examples of the keenest sort." An important contribution to the canon of Clough criticism.

1920
"A Study of Clough," *TLS* March 4 1920 p 153   **275**
In this incisive review, the writer points out the shortcomings of Osborne's study of Clough (No 273), particularly his disinclination to "dwell on the positive qualities of Clough's poetry," and he himself stresses the underlying appeal of Clough's work: "a fidelity of thought and feeling which is uncommon and wears well." Another point he makes bears repetition: "If Matthew Arnold's view of poetry as a criticism of life applies to anyone, it certainly applies to Clough."

Elton, Oliver. *Survey of English Literature, 1780–1880* (4 vols, New York 1920) iii 260, 302; iv 3 96–97, 313, 318, 376   **276**

Krutch, Joseph Wood. "Log of a Spiritual Voyage" [Review of No 273] *The Bookman* (New York) li (Aug 1920) 687–689   **277**

Roberts, R. E.   "Thrysis" [Review of No 273] *The Bookman* (London) LVIII (April 1920) 23–24   **278**

Acknowledging that "Thrysis" gives an incomplete idea of its subject, Roberts emphasizes the modernity of Clough, particularly praising his depiction of the self-analytic, egotistic Claude, the hero of *Amours de Voyage,* who resembles the hero of a modern novel.

S[tokoe,] F. W.   "Dipsychus" [Review of No 273] *The Athenaeum* No 4687 (Feb 27 1920) 268–269   **279**

1921

Gosse, Sir Edmund.   "Arthur Hugh Clough," *Books on the Table* (London 1921) 127–135   **280**

V[an] D[oren], M[ark]   "Arthur Hugh Clough" [Review of No 273] *Nation* (New York) CXII (Jan 26 1921) 122–123   **281**

1922

Hewlett, Maurice Henry.   "Teufelsdröckh in Hexameters," *Nineteenth Century and After* XCI (Jan 1922) 68–75; reprinted in *Extemporary Essays* (London 1922) p 176–187   **282**

A good account of the Carlylian elements in the *Bothie* and the particular use Clough makes of them.

1923

Cazamian, Madeleine.   *Le Roman et les Idées en Angleterre* (3 vols, Strasbourg 1923) I 260–261   **283**

Drinkwater, John.   *Victorian Poetry* (London 1923) 82, 84   **284**

Williams, S. T.   "Clough's Prose," *Studies in Victorian Literature* (London 1923) 235–252   **285**

An essay to be read in conjunction with Beatty's (No 289). Williams, unlike Beatty, finds that Clough's prose is stylistically undistinguished; it is laborious, self-conscious, conventional, lacks charm. Capable writing, nothing more, it deserves to be forgotten except for one point: its relation to Clough's inmost thought. (Part II of this bibliography indicates its greater range and value.)

1924

Hoyt, Arthur S.   *The Spiritual Message of Modern English Poetry* (New York 1924) 185–195   **286**

Kimbro, Gladys Mae.   "Arthur Hugh Clough," Master's Essay, University of Oklahoma 1924   **287**

1925

Knickerbocker, W. S.   *Creative Oxford: Its Influence in Victorian Literature* (New York 1925) 94–98   **288**

1926

Beatty, Joseph M., Jr.   "Arthur Hugh Clough as Revealed in His Prose," *South Atlantic Quarterly* xxv (April 1926) 168–180   **289**

One of the few studies devoted exclusively to Clough's prose, concentrating on his letters but touching on his essays and lectures. In discussing the content, the author makes a good case for the Straussian influence on Clough's religious thought and skilfully traces his advance from spiritual introspection to concern for social welfare. Clough's prose style is praised for its intellectual cast, balance, impeccable taste, equability of temper. (Cf No 285.)

Sprague, Janet Gilbertine. "Arthur Hugh Clough in Relation to the Victorian Doubt," Williams Memorial Prize Essay, University of Rochester 1926. Typescript of 17 pages, plus a one-page bibliograhy **290**
After reviewing political and religious reform movements of the 1830s and 1840s, the author cites some of Clough's poems to show the pathos of his carrying "suspension of judgment to the verge of futility."

1927

Cazamian, Louis. *A History of English Literature*, tr from the French by W. D. MacInnes and the author (New York 1927) II 339, 385–386, 387 [3] **291**

Knickerbocker, W. S. "Matthew Arnold at Oxford," *Sewanee Review* xxxv (Oct 1927) 399–418 **292**

Sams, Vera E. "Arthur Hugh Clough: A Study of His Thought," Master's Essay, University of Texas 1927 **293**

1928

Fehr, Bernhard. *Die englische Literatur des 19. und 20. Jahrhunderts* (Wildpark-Potsdam 1928) 189–190 **294**

Gobrecht, W. R. "Is There a God?" *The Gospel Message in Great Poems* (New York 1928) 161–175 **295**

Grierson, H. J. C. *Lyrical Poetry from Blake to Hardy* (London 1928) 96 **296**

Stet. [Welby, T. E.] "Back Numbers, LXXVIII," *The Saturday Review* cxlv (June 23 1928) 805; reprinted as "Clough" in his *Back Numbers* (London 1929) 106–110 **297**

1929

Lucas, F. L. "Thyrsis," *Life and Letters Today* II (May 1929) 344–360; same as "Clough," *Eight Victorian Poets* (Cambridge 1930) 55–74; *Ten Victorian Poets* (1940) 55–74 **298**
This superficial essay abounds in destructive statements made in well-turned phrases: Clough suffered from "Rugbeian elephantiasis of the conscience"; "This child of Diffidence was bred up to Too-good, then sent to live in Doubting Castle"; "He *is* Hamlet, Hamlet with a touch of Polonius — not Shakespeare."

McCormick, Mary E. "Arnold and Clough: A Comparative Study of Religious Thought," Master's Essay, Cornell 1929 **299**

Meissner, Paul. "Pessimistische Strömungen im englischen Geistesleben des 19. Jahrhunderts," *Englische Studien* lxiv (1929) 445 **300**

Turner, Albert Morton. "A Study of Clough's *Mari Magno*," *PMLA* xliv (June 1929) 569–589 **301**
An investigation of the autobiographical elements and the influence of Chaucer and Crabbe in these last poems of Clough.

[3] The first volume of this book is by Emile Legouis.

Weatherhead, Thomas E. *The Afterworld of the Poets* . . . (London 1929) 144–
153   *302*

1930

Kent, Muriel. "A Balliol Scholar," *Criterion* ix (July 1930) 675–688   *303*

Krahmer, Alfred John. "Arthur Hugh Clough in America," Master's Essay,
Columbia 1930   *304*

Wright, H. G. "Clough and Wales," *Welsh Outlook*, July 1930, p 194–195   *305*

1931

Garrod, H. W. "Clough," *Poetry and the Criticism of Life* (Cambridge, Mass
1931) 109–127   *306*

Gredler, Hazel, R. "Arthur Hugh Clough: A Character Study," Master's Essay
Cornell 1931   *307*

King, Carlyle. "Arthur Hugh Clough: A Critical Study," Doct Diss University of
Toronto 1931   *308*

MacCarthy, Desmond. "Clough," *Portraits* (London 1931) 63–67 (In the dedica-
tion MacCarthy indicates that the essay was written earlier.)   *309*
   Criticizing the derogatory judgments of both Swinburne and Strachey (Nos 178 and 267),
MacCarthy finds Clough "a man of strong will, a steady man with an unusual power of persistence
and self-control; he was more like a muscle-bound athlete than a weakling in respect of will
power." As poet, MacCarthy finds Clough "unique" in his own time, particularly in his fidelity
to facts and his refusal to heighten his own feelings. "We ought to be thankful he did not ride
off like his contemporaries on the high horse of some prophetic cause, or even on Pegasus." An
important corrective to much of the unfavorable and misleading criticism about Clough.

1932

Doorn, Willem van. *Theory and Practice of English Narrative Verse since 1833*
(Amsterdam 1932) 116–127   *310*

Lowry, H. F. "Introduction," to *The Letters of Matthew Arnold to Arthur Hugh
Clough* (Oxford 1932) 1–53 (See No 13 for the letters)   *311*
   Lowry's introductory essay not only provides a deeper insight into the relationship between
the two poets, but makes an important contribution to a better appreciation of Clough's character and thought. He stresses Clough's claim to the name of poet and critic, analyzes his moral
and aesthetic ideas, and indicates the extent of Clough's influence on his younger friend, which
is perhaps greater than most scholars have realized. "The depth [in Arnold] was, to be sure,
already there; it only needed sounding. And in this last work Clough unquestionably had a part."

Peake, L. S. "A. H. Clough as a Religious Teacher," *Modern Churchman* xxii
(July 1932) 191–199   *312*
   A rewarding discussion of Clough's attitude towards nature, God, pain and evil, duty, and
immortality. The analysis of Clough's concept of duty is of special value.

Wolfe, Humbert. "Arthur Hugh Clough," in *The Eighteen-Sixties* ed John Drinkwater (London 1932) 20–50   *313*
   Dwelling on the unfulfilled promise that many saw in Clough, Wolfe supplies his own thesis
as to why it remained unfulfilled. It was not religious difficulty. What absorbed and finally
destroyed him was the struggle of "the innate satirical genius seeking in vain to rid itself of the
swaddling-clothes of Arnoldism, and of all the honourable and clogging pieties of the period."

1933

"Arnold and Clough," *TLS*, Jan 12 1933 p 13–14   **314**

Bonnerot, Louis. [Review of No 311] *Revue Anglo-Américaine* x (Aug 1933) 532–533   **315**

B[randl,] A. [Review of No 311] *Archiv für das Studium der Neuren Sprachen* CLXIV (1933) 138–139   **316**

Dodds, J. W. "Arnold and Clough" [Review of No 311] *Virginia Quarterly Review* IX (July 1933) 453–457   **317**

Harris, Alan. "Matthew Arnold: The Unknown Years," *Nineteenth Century and After* CXIII (April 1933) 498–509   **318**

Hartwell, R. M. "Arthur Hugh Clough: An Impression of a Victorian," Master's Essay, McGill 1933   **319**

Holloway, Owen E. "Clough and Oriel," *TLS*, March 23 1933, p 200   **320**

Kingsmill, Hugh. "Matthew Arnold and Arthur Clough" [Review of No 311] *The English Review* LVI (Feb 1933) 227–230   **321**

Knickerbocker, W. A. "Semaphore: Arnold and Clough," *Sewanee Review* XLI (April 1933) 152–174 (Concerned with No 311)   **322**

Trilling, Lionel. "The Youth of Arnold," *Nation* CXXXVI (Feb 22 1933) 211 (Cf No 339)   **323**

The decided change in Arnold from an "enormously and attractively alive and unhampered" individual to the "unattractive," the "dull, unsparkling person of mediocre emotions" found in the Russell letters seems to Trilling clearly discernible in the correspondence published by Lowry, and the crisis that occurred in his friendship with Clough is the symbol of that change. "Clough was the symbol of Arnold's youth, and Clough, with his fluctant doubts, was inviting the world to kill him, spiritually and materially, while Arnold was trying to make himself at home in that world."

Winwar, Frances. *Poor Splendid Wings* (Boston 1933) 324   **324**

Young, Karl. "Matthew Arnold," *Saturday Review of Literature* IX (April 15 1933) 539   **325**

Reviewing the Lowry edition of the Arnold-Clough letters, Young traces three phases of their friendship: first, Clough attempted to regulate the "intellectual waywardness" of Matt; second, Arnold assumed the master's rod; third, a "quiet estrangement" hovered over their friendship.

Zabel, Morton D. "Corydon to Thyrsis," *Commonweal* XVII (April 5 1933) 640–641   **326**

For Zabel, the *Letters to Clough* shows that Clough was to Arnold "a mirror of his own profoundest problems."

1934

Cunliffe, John W. "Mid-Victorian Poets," in *Leaders of the Victorian Revolution* (New York 1934) 235–236   **327**

1936

"Arthur Hugh Clough," in *Bibliographies of Twelve Victorian Authors*, compiled by T. G. Ehrsam and R. H. Deily, under the direction of R. M. Smith (New York 1936) 68–75   **328**

Roberts, Michael, ed. "Introduction," to *The Faber Book of Modern Verse* (London 1936) 11–14 (Cf No 498)   **329**

Quotes selections from *Amours de Voyage* to illustrate the modernity of Clough's poetry; shows some specific resemblances in tone, intention, and "metaphysical" quality to the poetry of Pound and Eliot.

Scudder, Townsend. "Incredible Recoil: A Study in Aspiration," *American Scholar* v (Winter 1936) 35–48; reprinted in slightly different form in *The Lonely Wayfaring Man* (London 1936) 154–167   **330**

An imaginative re-creation of Emerson's high expectations of his English friend aroused by his reading of the *Bothie*, and his subsequent grief and disappointment at his later failure, the victim of an "extraordinary recoil," who passed, defeated, "through the portals of his own dissolution." Emerson could only ponder "the amazing aspiration, the amazing retreat," both so evident in the poem *Amours de Voyage*, the ending of which was to him so unsatisfying. Some of the imaginative deductions arrived at by the author have been corrected by subsequent publications, but the essay retains interest as a critical *tour de force*.

1937

Bush, Douglas. *Mythology and the Romantic Tradition in English Poetry* (Cambridge, Mass 1937) 274–275   **331**

Routh, H. V. *Towards the Twentieth Century* (New York 1937) 156, 167–170 **332**

As far as Routh is concerned, Clough "resigned himself" when he resigned Oxford; his university career sapped his inspiration, unsettled his thoughts, and oppressed his buoyancy and creativeness. Accordingly, the *Bothie*, the only poem of Clough's that Routh believes worth any consideration, takes on great significance; it becomes a symbol of Clough's own life, partly because it is full of promise, and partly because that promise was not fulfilled. The other poems have some excellent ideas and passages, but "none of them really expresses what the poet was feeling." For this critic, then, Clough "sacrificed his literary career to this concentrated lack of concentration."

1938

"Clough, the Minor Prophet: (A Victim of Victorian *Malaise*)" [Review of No 334] *TLS*, Oct 8 1938, p 638   **333**

Levy, Goldie. *Arthur Hugh Clough: 1819–1861* (London 1938)   **334**

An important biographical study of Clough, not superseded by Lady Chorley's (No 459), supplying details of his movements during most of his life, and utilizing much contemporary material. Of no critical value.

MacCarthy, Desmond. "The Modern Poet," *The Sunday Times* (London), Dec 25 1938, p 6   **335**

In this brief notice of Goldie Levy's biography, MacCarthy's judgment that Clough was not a great poet, but a "rare" one whose contribution to English poetry is "unique and valuable" is refreshing. He refutes the so-called "failure" of Clough; points out the similar difficulties faced by Clough and our modern poets, and how the former met them; and emphasizes the fact that Clough wrote some noteworthy poetry.

1939

Bonnerot, Louis. [Review of No 334] *Etudes Anglaises* iii (July 1939) 275–276   **336**

Largely unfavorable; Bonnerot notes the fine bibliography and wealth of biographical detail, but he contests the main thesis of the study — i.e., "Clough is more interesting than his poetry."

Trilling sees Arnold's "long sad personal" battle with Clough, fought "under a cloak of aesthetic discussion," as a battle against the "driving restless movement of the critical intellect." Knowing that his own poetic genius was not of the greatest, Arnold perceived that it had to be protected against the "incapacitating force" which Clough represented. Hence arose their debate on poetry and poetic theory, of which, unfortunately, we have only one side preserved in Lowry's edition of the letters. This first chapter of Trilling's study provides excellent insight into the attitude of the early aesthetically inclined Arnold towards his older friend. To Arnold, Clough's poetry is too much "of the head"; he is too much of a "mere d——d depth hunter in poetry" and not enough of that cherished ideal of the early Arnold — the *artist*.

To be a failure here means to be a sceptic, especially in religion. So defined, Palmer answers the title question negatively. A "disproportionate" emphasis has been given, he thinks, to Clough's sceptical habit of mind, and his classification as a doubter is, at best, a half-truth. Through a study of Clough's longer poems, particularly the later *Mari Magno,* and his letters and essays, Palmer demonstrates that Clough held positive moral convictions and positive social attitudes, and that he gave them full expression in his work and in his own life. The essay is one answer to those critics who would follow that tradition that labels Clough a failure.

1944

Palmer, Francis W.   "The Bearing of Science on the Thought of Arthur Hugh Clough," *PMLA* LIX (March 1944) 212–225   *350*

Palmer shows that Clough was not unaware of the scientific movements of his day. He traces the poet's interest in scientific investigation, the importance he assigned to objectivity, his concern for Biblical criticism, his evolutionary outlook, and his "modern" religious viewpoint. The analysis of *Natura Naturans* in relation to evolution is important.

1945

Benét, W. R.   "The Phoenix Nest," *Saturday Review of Literature* XXVIII (Jan 20 1945), 40–41   *351*

Benét cites a letter from Eric Underwood telling of the presentation of a bust of Clough to the City Hall of Charleston, S.C.

Bibliographies of Studies in Victorian Literature . . . 1932–1944, ed W. D. Templeman (Urbana 1945)   *352*

Mulhauser, Frederick, Jr.   "Clough's 'Love and Reason,'" *MP* XLII (Nov 1945) 174–186   *353*

Using three unpublished versions and the final published one of this poem, Mulhauser makes two important points. First, he supplies at least a partial answer to those critics who dismiss Clough's love lyrics as "impersonal, stilted, intellectualized" by showing the process by which this one became transformed in both language and intent from a personal consideration of the best time for a young man to marry into an intellectualized and philosophical discussion of the relation between love and reason. Second, he sheds some badly needed light on Clough's method of poetic composition.

Underwood, Eric.   "A. H. Clough," *TLS* Sept 8 1945 p 427   *354*

1947

Bishop, Morchard.   "Thyrsis; or, the Importance of Not Being Earnest," in *The Pleasure Ground,* ed Malcolm Elwin (London 1947) 61–74   *355*

Bonnerot, Louis.   *Matthew Arnold, "Empédocle sur L'Etna"* ("*Empedocles on Etna*"), *étude critique et traduction* (Paris 1947) 63–68, on similarities and differences between *Dipsychus* and *Empedocles*   *356*

—— *Matthew Arnold, Poète: Essai de Biographie Psychologique* (Paris 1947) *passim,* esp 20–29, 454–458, 477–482   *357*

Etherington, M.   "Clough at Oxford," *Church Quarterly Review* CXXXIV (July 1947) 184–195   *358*

Turner, Paul.   "*Dover Beach* and *The Bothie of Tober-na-Vuolich*," *English Studies* XXVIII (Dec 1947) 173–178 (Cf No 366)   *359*

1948

Chew, Samuel C. "Matthew Arnold and Arthur Hugh Clough," in A *Literary History of England*, ed A. C. Baugh (New York 1948) 1405–1407 **360**

McAllaster, Elva Arline. "Arthur Hugh Clough," in "The Oxford Movement and Victorian Poetry," Doct Diss University of Illinois 1948. Pages 99–113, 276 **361**

Norrington, A. L. P. "Say not, the struggle nought availeth," *Essays . . . Presented to Sir Humphrey Milford* (Oxford 1948) 29–41 **362**

1949

Yeoman, John R. H. "Mr. MacNeice's Poems," *TLS* Nov 18 1949 p 751 **363**

The writer sees a similarity between the *Bothie* and MacNeice's *Autumn Journal,* and he is puzzled why so few people seem to appreciate either. "Here are two simple unpretentious poems — quietly charming and occasionally moving — which maintain an evenly good standard throughout." The similarity of Clough and various modern poets is being noticed by many critics: see in particular Nos 329, 373, 376, 392, 498, and 500.

1950

Heath-Stubbs, John. *The Darkling Plain* (London 1950) 108–111 **364**

Macdonald, Isobel. "Victorian Verse Novels," *Listener* Mar 16 1950 p 485–486 **365**

Trawick, Buckner, B. "The Sea of Faith and the Battle by Night in *Dover Beach*," *PMLA* lxv (Dec 1950) 1282–83 (Cf No 359) **366**

1951

Badger, Kingsbury. "Arthur Hugh Clough as Dipsychus," *Modern Language Quarterly* xii (March 1951) 39–56 **367**

Brewster, Joan. "Arthur Hugh Clough: His Thought and Art," Master's Essay, University College, University of London 1951 **368**

Buckley, J. H. *The Victorian Temper* (Cambridge, Mass 1951) 26, 52, 107–108, 110, 116, 235 **369**

Dalglish, Doris N. "A Minor Victorian Masterpiece," *The Friends' Quarterly* v (July 1951) 170–181 **369a**

The "masterpiece" is *Dipsychus*.

Johari, G. P. "Arthur Hugh Clough at Oriel and at University Hall," *PMLA* lxvi (June 1951) 405–425 **370**

The author supplies further information about Clough's years at Oxford and University Hall. He shows conclusively that Clough's resignation from Oxford was of his own choice, but that his departure from University Hall was not. His services were terminated because the Council felt the affairs of the Hall were not prospering under Clough's direction. Especially helpful in revealing Clough's difficulties with the members of the Council on moral and religious questions.

Lovelace, R. E. "Wordsworth and the Early Victorians," Doct Diss University of Wisconsin 1951 **371**

Norrington, A. L. P. "Preface" to *The Poems of Arthur Hugh Clough*, ed H. F.
Lowry, A. L. P. Norrington, and F. L. Mulhauser (Oxford 1951) v–xiv   **372**

The "Preface" consists of a very brief biographical sketch, a chronological listing of the
published editions of Clough's poetry, an explanation of the editorial practices and standards
followed by the editors of the 1951 edition, and a discussion and analysis of Clough's hexameters.
(See Part I, No 99, for a critical comment on the 1951 edition.)

Pritchett, V. S. "Books in General," *New Statesman and Nation* XLI n.s. (Jan 6
1951) 15–16; same as "The Poet of Tourism" in *Books in General* (London 1953)
1–6   **373**

Pritchett, in an appreciative essay on *Amours de Voyage*, cites Clough as one of the few Victorians who seem to belong to our time rather than their own.

Robertson, D. A., Jr. "Clough's 'Say Not' in MS," *N&Q* Nov 10 1951 499–500 (See
Part I, No 81)   **374**

—— " 'Dover Beach' and 'Say Not,' " *PMLA* LXVI (Dec 1951) 919–928. (Receipt
of the offprint of this article noted by the editor in *N&Q* March 1 1952 p 104.) **375**

"The Poetry of Clough," *TLS* Nov 23 1951 p 748   **376**

The reviewer of the 1951 edition of the *Poems* emphasizes Clough's modernity, particularly
evident in *Dipsychus* and *Mari Magno*. In his own way Clough, like Browning in another, "admit-
ted more of the quality of coinage of prose into the currency of poetry." More important, this
technique was a deliberate one, rather than an "exercise" in the tradition of *Don Juan*; it was
"a serious integrity of art" regarded as bound, and indeed solely existing, to reveal a psychological stage of human imagination. An important article in recent criticism of Clough.

Woodham-Smith, Cecil. *Florence Nightingale* (New York 1951) *passim*   **377**

1952 [4]

Abercrombie, Ralph. "Clough" [Review of the *Poems*] *Spectator* CLXXXVIII (Jan 18
1952) 86   **378**

Abercrombie takes issue with the commonly held notion of Clough as an "earnest eminent
Victorian." Lytton Strachey's account of Clough (No 267) is "a vulgar travesty, based obviously
on distorted secondhand evidence." There are dull stretches in Clough, but he also at times
comes to life and writes with "an adult irony and intelligence, a vivacious wordly feeling for
reality" that must confound anyone who thinks of him as a prig.

Baum, Paull. "Clough and Arnold," *Modern Language Notes* LXVII (Dec 1952)
546–547   **379**

Curvegnen, John. "Theodore Walrond: Friend of Arnold and Clough," *Durham
University Journal* XLIV (March 1952) 56–61   **380**

Dalglish, Doris N. "Arthur Hugh Clough: The Shorter Poems," *Essays in Criticism* II (Jan 1952) 38–53   **381**

The author is surprised by the neglect into which the shorter poems have fallen and is exas-
perated at seeing "so much rough-hewn excellence, even loveliness lying unread." Her inconclusive findings from an examination of his religious poems are far from satisfactory; her conclusions about his lyrics on friendship and his satiric pieces on society and human nature are
more convincing. Worth repeating is her advice on the proper approach to his lyrics: "With
much of Clough's poetry a second or a third reading is necessary before one can dig through the

[4] The *Poems* under review in this year and the next is the 1951 edition referred to in No 372.

sheer solidity of thought and discover the spring of imagination. He demands concentrated reading, for he usually lacks surface attention."

Mack, Edward C., and W. H. G. Armytage. *Thomas Hughes: The Life of the Author of Tom Brown's Schooldays* (London 1952) 15, 29, 41, 42, 73   **382**

Maison, Margaret. "Poetic Melancholy: A Study of Alfred Tennyson, Matthew Arnold, and Arthur Hugh Clough," Master's Essay, King's College, University of London 1952   **383**

[Review of the *Poems*] *The Listener* XLVII (April 24 1952) 682, 685   **384**

[Review of the *Poems*] In "Reviews," *Durham University Journal* XLIV (March 1952) 75–76   **385**
Clough emerges decisively as "a poet of rank," for his major poems are full of positive virtues. *Dipsychus*, with its gusto, range of mood, humour, and understanding of the heart of man, will probably be counted as his masterpiece.

Schmezer, Guido. *Das poetische Genus in den Gedichten von Matthew Arnold und Arthur Hugh Clough*, Inaugural Dissertation (Berne 1952)   **386**
The author examines twenty-five categories of words, such as earth, nature, water, life, death, soul, destiny, hope, fame, to see what "gender" each poet uses with that word; because of the limited samplings and the uncritical approach the study is of limited value.

Townsend, F. G. "Clough's 'The Struggle': The Text, Title, and Date of Publication," *PMLA* LXVII (Dec 1952) 1191–92. (See Part I, No 81)   **387**

Willey, Basil. "Books in General," *New Statesman and Nation*, XLIII n.s. (Jan 26 1952) 100–101   **388**
Following the lead of the critical tradition, Willey uses the occasion of reviewing the 1951 *Poems* to compare Clough with Arnold, to the former's disadvantage. Clough "suffered all his life from an incapacity to make up his mind," and his life and work leave upon us the impression of unfulfilled promise.

1953
Berlind, Bruce. "A Curious Accomplishment," *Poetry* LXXXII (April 1953) 27–34   **389**
In this review of the 1951 *Poems*, Berlind laments the poet's lack of an "objective grip" on reality that would have given him better artistic control, and he cites "Blessed are those who have not seen" as an example that reveals this particular defect. The poet's ambivalent attitude, so clearly depicted in the poem, prevents any "total attitude" from emerging. Yet, the reviewer concludes: "Perhaps the ultimate twinge of dissatisfaction . . . is in part a sense of guilt at our own facile disregard of that second thought."

Garrod, H. W. [Review of the *Poems*] *RES* IV n.s. (Jan 1953) 81–83   **390**

"Gift of Manuscripts of Poetical Works of A. H. Clough," *Bodleian Library Record* IV (1953) 289–290   **391**

Jump, J. D. "Clough's *Amours de Voyage*," *English* IX (Summer 1953) 176–178   **392**
The author calls the poem "a minor masterpiece," one of the finest and most readable longer poems of the Victorian age. Viewing it as a serio-comic novel in verse, he finds its merits in the

freedom and confidence with which the hexameter form is handled, the skilful characterization of the protagonist, and the treatment of theme in a serio-comic vein instead of the nineteenth-century tradition of "elevated" poetry.

Maxwell, J. C. "Arnold's Letters to Clough: A Correction," *N&Q* Oct 1953 p 440
393

Norrington, A. L. P. "Clough and *In Memoriam*," *RES* IV n.s. (Oct 1953) 364 **394**

Rudman, H. W. "Clough: 'Say not the Struggle,'" *N&Q* June 1953 p 261–263
(See Part I, No 81) **395**

Tillotson, Kathleen. "Rugby 1850: Arnold, Clough, Walrond, and *In Memoriam*," *RES* IV n.s. (April 1953) 122–140 (See No 215) **396**

Tompkins, J. M. S. [Review of the *Poems*] *Modern Language Review* XLVIII (April 1953) 206–207 **397**

For Tompkins, the accurate and complete texts of the poems, particularly of *Dipsychus*, help us to see all sides of Clough, rather than only that emphasized by Arnold in *Thyrsis*. "Clough is worth remembering in his totality, for his satire, his gaiety with the thread of twisted steel in it, for the 'spoken' note of his varied verse, . . . and for the plain, exact and often conversational diction, which [his contemporaries] found insufficiently elevated."

1954
"Master and Pupils," *TLS* June 18 1954 p 397 [Review of No 401] **398**

[Review of Frances Woodward's *The Doctor's Disciples*] *N&Q* Aug 1954 p 368
399

The reviewer disagrees with some of the author's statements about Clough's poetry and life: "He cannot agree that some verses of Clough to his wife were doggerel. He cannot agree that Clough's eventual finding of a sphere of humble usefulness . . . was a declension from writing more poems."

Tillotson, Geoffrey. "New Verses by Arthur Hugh Clough," *TLS* June 18 1954
400 **400**

Commentary on some translations contained in an article by Clough entitled "Illustrations of Latin Lyrical Metres." (See Part II, No 20)

Woodward, Frances. "Arthur Hugh Clough," *The Doctor's Disciples* (London 1954) Chap III p 127–179 **401**

A rapid survey of Clough's life and work that is largely unfavorable in its conclusions. The author finds Dr Arnold's influence on the young Clough an enervating one; she agrees with F. L. Lucas and Osborne that Newmanism and Ward were difficulties too great for Clough to overcome, and that at Oxford his position was "irreparably undermined"; and she believes that his last years were spent in drudgery, a poor ending to a life of little "positive achievement."

1955
Jump, J. D. *Matthew Arnold* (London 1955) *passim*, esp p 24–32 **402**

1956
Allott, Kenneth. "An Arnold-Clough Letter: References to Carlyle and Tennyson," *N&Q* June 1956 p 267 **403**

Bertram, J. "The Ending of Clough's *Dipsychus*," *RES* vii n.s. (Jan 1956) 59–
  60   **404**

Bibliographies of Studies in Victorian Literature . . . 1945–1954, ed Austin Wright
  (Urbana 1956)   **405**

Johnson, W. Stacy. "Parallel Imagery in Arnold and Clough," *English Studies*
  xxxvii (Feb 1956) 1–11   **406**
  Shows by numerous quotations that Arnold and Clough seem to have carried on a kind of
  correspondence or debate in poetic form and affirms that the two poets were more important to
  each other poetically than has often been thought.

Terhune, A. McKinley. "Arthur Hugh Clough," *The Victorian Poets: A Guide to
  Research*, ed F. E. Faverty (Cambridge, Mass 1956) 104–110; revised by
  M. Timko in 1967   **407**

Tillotson, Kathleen. "Matthew Arnold and Carlyle," *Proceedings of the British
  Academy* xlii (London 1956) 133–153 (esp 137)   **408**

Timko, Michael. "The Lyrics of Arthur Hugh Clough: Their Background and
  Form," Doct Diss University of Wisconsin 1956   **409**

Willey, Basil. *More Nineteenth-Century Studies* (London 1956) 44, 45, 107, 114
                                                                                410
1957
Cockshut, A. O. J. [Review of *Correspondence*] *Manchester Guardian*, Dec 10
  1957 p 4   **411**

Fairchild, Hoxie N. ""Clough," *Religious Trends in English Poetry* (New York
  1957) iv (1830–1880) Chap xviii 505–527   **412**
  The chapter devoted to Clough portrays the spiritual difficulties the poet experienced in his
  life and depicted in his poetry; but Clough's religious development and final position are blurred
  by the author's method of bringing in quotations from various poems without any regard to dates
  and periods in which they were written and juxtaposing the ideas found in them. To be understood, Clough's religious poetry needs to be placed in the context of his life and thought (cf Nos
  114 and 446).

Faber, Geoffrey. *Jowett: A Portrait with Background* (Cambridge, Mass 1957)
  30, 108, 112, 126n2, 126–127, 160, 188, 306, 316, 333–334, 335 (See Nos 6, 12) **413**

Gollin, Richard M. "Arthur Hugh Clough," *Cambridge Bibliography of English
  Literature*, supplementary volume, ed George Watson (Cambridge 1957) v
  589–590   **414**

Houghton, Walter E. *The Victorian Frame of Mind, 1830–1870* (New Haven
  1957) 106–109; and see index   **415**

Howard, William. "Clough's Say not the Struggle Naught[sic] Availeth," *Expli-
  cator* (March 1957) item 59 (See Part I, No 81)   **416**

"If His Hopes Were Dupes Fears May Be Liars," *The Times* (London) Oct 31
  1957 p 13   **417**

Macaulay, Rose. "Victorian 'Angst'," *The Listener* LVIII (Dec 5 1957) 937   *418*

In her review of the *Correspondence* she decides that Clough was a highly intelligent versifier, a prig in a quite pleasant sense, and a fairly entertaining letter writer.

Mulhauser, F. L. "Introduction" to *The Correspondence of Arthur Hugh Clough,* ed F. L. Mulhauser (2 vols, Oxford 1957) I xiii–xxiii (See No 7 for comment on the letters)   *419*

Rather than attempting to come to any definite conclusions about Clough's life and work in his introductory essay to the *Correspondence,* the editor is more interested in pointing out various aspects that need further study. He suggests, for instance, the qualities of Clough's personality that need more consideration: his shyness and conscientiousness; he finds that the motives for Clough's resignation from Oxford were more complicated than has generally been supposed; and, contrary to many criticisms of Clough's life, he believes that the poet did achieve during his last years a pattern of living that brought him satisfaction.

Nicolson, Harold. "Say Not the Struggle . . . ," *The Observer* (London) Dec 15 1957 p 12   *420*

To Nicolson, reviewing the *Correspondence,* the enigma of Clough is unsolved. "His character remains a fascinating specimen of an unfulfilled prodigy."

Reid, J. C. *The Mind and Art of Coventry Patmore* (London 1957) 193, 325   *421*

Roll-Hansen, Diderik. *The Academy, 1869–1879* (Copenhagen 1957) 37, 134, 206, 207   *422*

[Tillotson, Geoffrey] "A Searcher for the Truth," *TLS* Dec 6 1957 p 738   *423*

This review of the *Correspondence* finds that the letters reveal Clough as "one of the most searching thinkers" of his time, and as a "strong man." Although on one occasion Clough referred to himself as "weak and yielding," it was in a "context that towered with strength." We must not make the mistake of judging him "merely on some of his acts." (The writer acknowledged the authorship in a personal letter to the editors.)

Spender, Stephen. "The Voice of Honest Doubt," in "Great Writers Rediscovered," *The Sunday Times* (London) Nov 3 1957 p 10   *424*

While Spender rightly states that Strachey's portrait of Clough (see No 267) is an unfair one, his own of Clough as "unhappily in love with the Arnolds, who played the role of God to him," and his interpretation of Clough's main poetic theme as a "kind of underground protest against them and their ideas about duty and beauty" are equally exaggerated. However, his analysis of Clough's poetic method and artistry is perceptive, his main point being that Clough was writing at a time when there was no characteristically "modernist" form into which he could fit his poetic ideas. It is against this background that Clough's willingness to sacrifice perfection of form for sincerity of vocabulary, his use of a language which "exactly conveys his temperament and his meaning, and which is idiomatically modern," should be seen. "His poetry and his case," Spender concludes, "do hold our attention: which means that on some level they are a success. . . . Briefly, Tennyson and Browning found forms which they sometimes used perfectly, but the very perfection of the forms inhibited them from using a contemporary idiom in which to convey contemporary experience or a discussion of disturbing current ideas."

1958
Allott, Kenneth. "Clough's Letters," *Essays in Criticism* VIII (Oct 1958) 438–446   *425*

In his review of the *Correspondence,* Allott presents a good analysis of the differences in editorial methods of Mrs Clough and Mulhauser, and the positive gains from those of the latter. He also asks if there is not a trace of ignominy in the "good sense" of contemporaries like Temple and Matthew Arnold when it is set beside Clough's "scrupulous drifting."

Gollin, R. M. "Sandford's Bid for the Edinburgh Professorship and Arthur Hugh Clough's Expectations," *N&Q* Nov 11 1958 p 470–472   *426*

Killham, John. *Tennyson and "The Princess"* (London 1948)   *427*
  Chapters V and VI on the feminist controversy provide valuable background for the *Bothie*, which is mentioned on p 118, 142.

Parkinson, Thomas. "The Correspondence of Arthur Hugh Clough," *Victorian Studies* I (June 1958) 367–369 [Review of the *Correspondence*]   *428*

Thompson, Lawrance. "A Hidden, Inner Life,' *New York Times Book Review* Jan 26 1958 p 4 [Review of the *Correspondence*]   *429*

Timko, Michael. [Review of the *Correspondence*] *Journal of English and Germanic Philology* LVII (Oct 1958) 825–829   *430*

Veyriras, Paul. "Un Regain d' Intérêt pour Arthur Hugh Clough," *Etudes Anglaises* XI (Juillet – Sept 1958) 226–228   *431*

Winther, S. K. [Review of the *Correspondence*] *Modern Language Quarterly* XIX (Sept 1958) 271–272   *432*

1959
Bertram, James. [Review of the *Correspondence*] *RES* X n.s. (Aug 1959) 313–316   *433*

Gollin, Richard M. "Arthur Hugh Clough: The Formative Years," Doct Diss University of Minnesota 1959; summary in *Dissertation Abstracts* XX (1959) 2276   *434*

Haight, Gordon S. [Review of the *Correspondence*] *Modern Language Review* LIV (Jan 1959) 103–104   *435*

Houghton, Walter E. "Arthur Hugh Clough," in *Victorian Poetry and Poetics*, ed W. E. Houghton and G. Robert Stange (Boston 1959) 336–340   *436*
  This short introduction to Clough's life and poetry indicates the important influences bearing on his thought and art; points out reasons for the past neglect of his work; and stresses the characteristics that made his poetry unique in his own time and make it "modern" in ours. Some of the extensive notes to the poems, pages 340–381, particularly those to *Uranus, Jacob*, and *Amours de Voyage*, are illuminating.

Polhemus, George W. "A Clough Epitaph," *N&Q* Feb 1959 p 65–66   *437*

Super, R. H. [Review of the *Correspondence*] *MP* LVI (Feb 1959) 213–215 *438*

Tener, Robert H. "Richard Holt Hutton," *TLS* April 24 1959 p 241   *439*

Timko, Michael. "Arthur Hugh Clough: A Portrait Retouched," *Victorian Newsletter* V (Spring 1959) 24–28   *440*

Trawick, Buckner B. "The Moon Metaphor in Browning's 'One Word More,'" *N&Q* Dec 1959, p 448 **441**

Vanderbilt, Kermit. *Charles Eliot Norton* (Cambridge, Mass 1959) 25, 49, 53, 59, 68, 79, 81, 178 **442**

1960
Houghton, Walter E. "The Prose Works of Arthur Hugh Clough: A Checklist and Calendar with Some Unpublished Passages," *Bulletin of the New York Public Library* LXIV (July 1960) 377–394 **443**
A supplement to this article forms Part II of the present catalogue.

Tener, R. H. "Clough, Hutton, and University Hall," *N&Q* Dec 1960 456–457 **444**

Timko, Michael. "*Amours de Voyage*: Substance or Smoke?" *English* XIII (Autumn 1960) 95–98; reprinted in revised form in No 500 (See also No 473 for another view of Claude.) **445**

—— "The 'True Creed' of Arthur Hugh Clough," *Modern Language Quarterly* XXI (Sept 1960) 208–222; reprinted in revised form in No 500 (For different views of Clough's "creed" see Nos 114 and 412.) **446**

1961
Allott, Kenneth. "Thomas Arnold the Younger, New Zealand, and the 'Old Democratic Fervour'," *Landfall* XV (Sept 1961) 208–225 **447**
The article contains some enlightening references to Clough's social and political views in the late forties.

Bertram, James. "Claude to Eustace, *Temps Modernes*: (After *Amours de Voyage*, by Arthur Hugh Clough)," *Landfall* XV (Sept 1961) 226–227 **448**

Black, Isabella. "Was It Arnold's Doing? A Psychological Study of Arthur Hugh Clough," *Psychoanalysis and the Psychoanalytic Review* XXXXVIII (Spring 1961) 104–110 **449**
The author's thesis is that Clough's admiration for Dr Arnold was a "positive factor in his development," not, as other critics have argued, a negative one. It is to the inadequacies of his relationships in his early home life that one must look for the source of Clough's "recognized limitations."

[Brasch, Charles] "Notes," *Landfall* XV (Sept 1961) 191–193 **450**
Some appreciative comments on the subject-matter and form of the *Bothie* and *Amours de Voyage.*

Green, David Bonnell. "Arthur Hugh Clough and Francis H. Underwood," *Victorian Newsletter* VII (Spring 1961) 15–17 **451**

Houghton, Walter E. "Arthur Hugh Clough: A Hundred Years of Disparagement," *Studies in English Literature* I (Autumn 1961) 35–61 **452**
A history of Clough's reputation designed to show why so fine a poet has been so persistently damned, or damned with faint praise, and thus to clear the ground for a fresh and open-minded reading of his poetry. Reprinted in revised form in No 473, Chapter I.

Rudman, Harry W. "Clough and Graham Greene's *The Quiet American*," *Victorian Newsletter* vii (Spring 1961) 14–15   ***453***

Timko, Michael. "Corydon Had a Rival," *Victorian Newsletter* vii (Spring 1961) 5–11   ***454***

A comparison of the poetic theories of Clough and Arnold indicates that they correspond at many points; Clough's influence on Arnold was greater than most critics are inclined to recognize. See also No 480.

1962

Allott, Kenneth. [Review of No 459] *Modern Language Review* lvii (July 1962) 428–429   ***455***

Alvarez, A. "Conviction of Excellence," *New Statesman and Nation* Feb 2 1962 p 163–164   ***456***

Armstrong, Isobel. *Arthur Hugh Clough* (London 1962). A pamphlet in the "Writers and Their Work" series, published for the British Council   ***457***

Burrows, L. R. "A Mid-Victorian Faust," *Westerly* i (Nov 1962) 97–106   ***458***

Chorley, Katharine. *Arthur Hugh Clough: The Uncommitted Mind* (Oxford 1962)   ***459***

An important biography of Clough which gives primary attention to the psychological disabilities that caused his notorious "failure." The treatment of Clough's art and thought is superficial. The author makes use of previously unpublished material, particularly the correspondence between Clough and Blanche; and she has discovered that *Dipsychus Continued* was written between December 1852 and June 1853.

"Dipsychus Unmasked" [Review of No 459] *TLS* Feb 2 1962 p 72   ***460***

Gollin, Richard M. "Clough Despite Himself" [Review of No 459] *Essays in Criticism* xii (Oct 1962) 426–435   ***461***

The opening pages of this severe review are a valuable description of the two Cloughs — the traditional image of man and poet versus the "real" image that is now coming into view. Believing Lady Chorley's picture of Clough to be radically misconceived, Gollin finds the psychological analyses irrelevant.

—— "The 1951 Edition of Clough's *Poems*: A Critical Re-Examination," *MP* lx (Nov 1962) 120–127 (See Part I, No 99.)   ***462***

Houghton, Walter E. [Review of No 459] *Victorian Studies* vi (Sept 1962) 91–92   ***463***

Lodge, David. "Religious Bitter" [Review of No 459] *Spectator* ccviii (Feb 16 1962) 214   ***464***

Nicolson, Harold. [Review of No 459] *The Observer* (London) Jan 14 1962 p 26   ***465***

Timko, Michael. "The Poetic Theory of Arthur Hugh Clough," *English Studies*
XLIII (Aug 1962) 240–247; reprinted in revised form in No 500   *466*

—— [Review of No 459] *Journal of English and Germanic Philology* LXI (Oct
1962) 937–940   *467*

Willey, Basil. [Review of No 459] *Listener* Feb 8 1962 p 261–262   *468*

1963
Bertram, James. "Clough and His Poetry," *Landfall* XVII (June 1963) 141–155 *469*

This review of Lady Chorley's biography (No 459) is also an appraisal of Clough as a
"modern" poet who has claims to our attention. See especially Bertram's support of *Amours de
Voyage* as Clough's masterpiece.

Borrie, M. A. F. "Three Poems of Arthur Hugh Clough," *British Museum Quarterly* XXVII (Autumn 1963) 9–11 (The three poems are "Bethesda. A Sequel,"
"The Latest Decalogue," and "O stream, descending to the sea.")   *470*

Brooks, Roger L. "The Genesis of Matthew Arnold's 'Thyrsis,'" *RES* XIV n.s.
(May 1963) 172–174. (See in reply Kenneth Allott's letter to the Editor, *RES* XV
n.s. (Aug 1964) 304–305.)   *471*

Green, D. B. "Arthur Hugh Clough and the Parkers," *N&Q* Jan 1963 p 24–26 *472*

Houghton, Walter E. *The Poetry of Clough: An Essay in Revaluation* (New
Haven 1963)   *473*

This critical study is intended to emphasize Clough's achievement as a poet and to stimulate
the reading of his work. After a history of the critical tradition [Cf No 452], it explores the
shorter poems in a long chapter on style and form, and then submits the five long poems to
fairly close analysis. The chapters on *Amours de Voyage* and *Dipsychus* are perhaps the most
important.

Mazzaro, Jerome L. "Corydon in Matthew Arnold's 'Thyrsis,'" *Victorian Poetry* I
(Nov 1963) 304–306   *474*

Ryals, Clyde De L. "An Interpretation of Clough's *Dipsychus*," *Victorian Poetry* I
(Aug 1963) 182–188   *475*

Drawing an analogy with the progress from "The Everlasting No" through "The Centre of
Indifference" to "The Everlasting Yea" in *Sartor Resartus*, Ryals sees the poem as an optimistic
record of development. The isolated and introspective Romantic finally learns the value of the
active life; and the conclusion, far from presenting the capitulation of the idealist to the hard
terms of the world, marks their wise "joining together." For another reading of the text see
No 473, Chap 6.

Timko, Michael. "The Satiric Poetry of Arthur Hugh Clough," *Victorian Poetry* I
(April 1963) 104–114; reprinted in slightly different form in No 500   *476*

1964
Allott, Kenneth. "Rescue Operation" [Review of No 473] *Essays in Criticism* XIV
(Oct 1964) 409–416   *477*

Badger, Kingsbury. [Review of No 473] *English Language Notes* I (June 1964) 310–312   **478**

Barish, Evelyn. "A New Clough Manuscript," *RES* xv n.s. (May 1964) 168–174
                                                                            479
Four additional previously unpublished stanzas of *"Solvitur Acris Hiems"* are discussed; they change the tone of the previously published three-stanza poem and further demonstrate the "modern" quality of Clough's poetry.

Brooks, Roger L. "Matthew Arnold's Revision of *Tristram and Iseult*: Some Instances of Clough's Influence," *Victorian Poetry* II (Winter 1964) 57–63 (See also No 454.)   **480**

Buckley, J. H. [Review of No 473] *Journal of English and Germanic Philology* LXIII (April 1964) 378–380   **481**

Cockshut, A. O. J. "Clough: The Real Doubter," in *The Unbelievers: English Agnostic Thought 1840–1890* (London 1964) 31–43 (See index for other references to Clough)   **482**
For Cockshut, Clough never developed any "coherent attitude" to religion, marriage, work, or life itself, and this failure is reflected in his poetry, in which he was unable to achieve "a grand, simple effect."

Coulling, Sidney. "Matthew Arnold's 1853 Preface: Its Origin and Aftermath," *Victorian Studies* VII (March 1964) 233–263   **483**

Culler, A. Dwight. [Review of No 473] *Yale Review* LIII (Spring 1964) 442 **484**

Hill, A. G. [Review of No 459] *RES* xv n.s. (Aug 1964) 332–334   **485**

McCarthy, Patrick. [Review of No 473] *Victorian Studies* VIII (March 1964) 316–317   **486**

Peattie, Roger W. "William Michael Rossetti," *TLS* July 30 1964 p 665 (See also No 49.)   **487**

"Shoring Up Victorian Stays" [Review of No 473] *TLS* Jan 9 1964 p 22   **488**

Timko, Michael. [Review of No 473] *Modern Language Quarterly* xxv (June 1964) 226–227   **489**

Tobias, Richard. [Review of No 473] *Victorian Poetry* II (Summer 1964) 209–211   **490**

Trawick, Buckner B., ed. "Introduction," in *Selected Prose Works of Arthur Hugh Clough* (University, Alabama 1964) 15–26   **491**
In his introductory comments Trawick emphasizes Clough's pre-eminence as a "thinker" and his complete intellectual honesty. His remarks on Clough's ideas about translation (p 20–21) are pertinent to a subject that needs further exploration. (See Kenneth Allott's severe review in *N&Q* Aug 1965 316–317.)

Veyriras, Paul. *Arthur Hugh Clough (1819–1861)* (Paris 1964: dated so but published in 1965)   ***492***

A large book (605 pages), and one containing a wealth of information on Clough's life and thought. While not extraordinarily illuminating on Clough's poetry (except for its remarks on the hexameter), this study is especially effective in depicting the milieu in which Clough lived and wrote. On the whole, Veyriras adheres to the "traditional" view of Clough the "failure."

Williamson, Eugene L. *The Liberalism of Thomas Arnold* (University, Alabama 1964) 21, 107, 210, 212, 213–216   ***493***

1965

Bowers, F. "Arthur Hugh Clough: Recent Revaluations," *Humanities Association Bulletin* (Canada) xvi (Fall 1965) 17–26   ***494***

A brief survey of recent trends in Clough criticism.

Green, D. B. [Review of No 473] *MP* lxii (May 1965) 367–368   ***495***

Miyoshi, Masao. "Clough's Poems of Self-Irony," *Studies in English Literature* v (Autumn 1965) 691–704   ***496***

"The Clough Context" [Review of No 492] *TLS* Dec 2 1965 p 1104   ***497***

1966

Bowers, Frederick. "Arthur Hugh Clough: the Modern Mind," *Studies in English Literature* vi (Autumn 1966) 709–716 (Cf No 329)   ***498***

For Bowers, Clough's work anticipates "in attitude and consequent tone" the best of twentieth century poetry; it is a return to "the intelligence of the line of wit which runs on to Eliot."

Castan, C. "Clough's 'Epi-Strauss-ium' and Carlyle," *Victorian Poetry* iv (Winter 1966) 54–56   ***499***

Timko, Michael. *Innocent Victorian: The Satiric Poetry of Arthur Hugh Clough.* (Ohio University Press 1966)   ***500***

Emphasizing what he calls Clough's "positive naturalism" or "moral realism," Timko discusses the poet's "liberal" ideas on economics, politics, society, and religion; he then stresses the satiric poetry as the means by which Clough was able to show with impressive artistry and great force how to overcome the difficulties faced by the age. The shorter satiric poems and the three important long ones — *The Bothie, Amours de Voyage,* and *Dipsychus* — are examined in terms of this positive naturalism, particularly the imagery. Includes a chronological bibliography of articles and books on Clough.

Index

TITLES or first lines of individual works by Clough are indexed (in italic). The index includes important references to Clough's writings but does not analyze tables of contents in collected works. There is no comprehensive index entry for Clough. Authors of critical works and the titles of all books are indexed but not titles of articles or book chapters. If an author has also been discussed in annotations, his name is given twice; large and small capitals indicate the subject entries. Numbers refer to entry items except where page ("p") is noted.